A CLOSER LOOK AT
POLITICAL COMMUNICATION

T0401295

POLITICAL SCIENCE AND HISTORY

POLITICAL SCIENCE AND HISTORY

A CLOSER LOOK AT
POLITICAL COMMUNICATION

MARK H. TATUM
EDITOR

nova
science publishers
New York

NOTICE TO THE READER

Library of Congress Cataloging-in-Publication Data

ISBN: 978-1-53615-321-7

Published by Nova Science Publishers, Inc. † New York

CONTENTS

PREFACE

Chapter one investigates how the local network media helps the key stakeholders to participate in the policy debate regarding a local low-income housing policy in Madison, Wisconsin, U.S.A., drawing mainly on Jürgen Habermas's theory of public sphere.

The second chapter discusses how coffee-houses and public reading houses are places today where political communication is often established, and the neighborhood effect is most often felt. It can be described not only as tea-coffee drinking places where free time is passed, but also as places where voter behavior begins to form and democracy is created.

The authors go on to focus on the past use of racialized language as one mechanism for evaluating political communication in the 21st century.

Lastly, the phenomenon of politicians employing prayer in the church as a potent political tool to subtly campaign for election and reelection in Nigeria is explored.

Chapter 1 - This study investigates how the local network media help the key stakeholders to participate in the policy debate regarding a local low-income housing policy in Madison, Wisconsin, U.S.A., drawing mainly on Jürgen Habermas's theory of public sphere. Particularly, it aims to localize Habermas's framework of social structure for local community-level research. It attempts to demonstrate why and how the rational model of the public sphere, which relies on rational and consensus-oriented public discourses, needs to be modified by showing how a contentious public sphere has emerged in the local network media space. With this framework and the research findings, it also discusses the media influence on local community leaders from the perspective of communication ecology.

Chapter 2 - Coffee-houses (*Kahvehane*) and Public Reading Houses (*Kıraathane*) are two public places where people enjoy their free time sipping their teas or coffees and talk about politics. In the Turkish society, since 1500s, during the reign of the Ottoman Empire, these two places have been spaces where politics is intensively discussed, decision is given for the selection of political power and where the government is criticized. In addition to being public reading house, the *Kıraathane* can be defined as a place where people have been enlightened from the past to the present, the political power is criticized where urban and rural life are united while drinking coffee and tea. These public reading houses are spaces open to the public in the ottoman empire during the reign of Suleyman the Magnificent, where the authority was thought to be weakened by means of the rumors in these places. On the other hand, the coffee-house is a place where the local people taste their coffee originally from Yemen and discuss how to overthrow the political power, discuss daily problems and make philosophical debates. During the Ottoman Empire, coffee houses were very often shut down in case riots could arise among the people by giving the excuse that coffee was not good for health and should be forbidden for religious reasons. Coffee-houses and public reading houses are places today where political communication is often established, and the neighborhood effect is most often felt. It can be described not only as tea-coffee drinking places where free time is passed, but also as places where voter behavior begins to form and democracy is created. In one study on coffee-houses, it is mentioned that in the 1960s there were not coffeehouses in the southeastern Anatolia in Turkey since the sheiks or leaders of the clans in the region did not want any opposition to their authority and rule. Based on this example, it is clear that the coffee-houses and public reading houses are spaces for political communication and democracy due to the neighborhood effect. It is also the place of the civil society where the citizens are expected to socialize. It is a place of letting the political culture live. In this respect, Kıraathane is a means of preserving the national values and local traditions. On the other hand, *Kahvehane* and *Kıraathane*, which are seen as leisure spots, are regarded as a demonstration of unemployment. Just as these spaces are a reflection of the economy, they are also projections of democracy in the public sphere. In the present work, after giving a historical background about the coffee-houses and public reading houses in Turkey, the authors will deal with the literature on these spaces from critical theory perspective of Jurgen Habermas. However, these public spaces are often gendered places in which men are predominant. They are places where men seek to give political decisions by talking to their friends. The neighborhood effect can therefore account for the voting behavior of women who are given less opportunity to participate in these spaces because of their gender. Thus, the authors will examine the public sphere, the voting behavior and the neighborhood effect by taking *Kahvehane* and *Kıraathane* as a case. The authors will consult the secondary sources in order to examine the case. In Turkey, the political power (ab)uses coffee-houses and public reading spaces as venues for their political campaigns. In fact, during the campaigns for the general elections on the 24th of June 2018, one of the commitments of the political power was on transforming the *Kıraathane* from places where only rumors are made into those where people read, learn and effect others while enjoying snacks for free.

Chapter 3 - The fiery language of Donald Trump – as both candidate and sitting president – regarding immigration and immigrants from Latin America (e.g., as rapists, murderers, invaders) has made headlines and sparked controversy. Characterizing illegal immigrants (and Latin people more broadly) in speeches, at rallies, and in the media in terms of violence, criminality, and as threats to national security, President Trump has been accused of employing a race-based crisis strategy to appeal to the fears and insecurities of white voters. However, to depict this type of political communication as somehow anomalous or otherwise unique to this administration and its specific goals misses the mark. Any effort to understand the key logics at play that make such a modern strategy both possible and potentially effective must place its analysis firmly within a larger historical context. Demonstrably, the usage of racialized metaphors - like invasion and infection – has been a cornerstone of United States policy towards those south of the border. Conceptions of Latin peoples as inferior and as a source of menace have been foundational elements of U.S. – Latin America relations throughout its nearly 200-year history. Clearly articulated in the Monroe Doctrine, these taken for granted themes figured prominently in a consistent foreign policy of direct and indirect interventions in the 19th and 20th centuries designed to ensure United States dominance within the hemisphere. Informed by a discourse theoretical methodology, this chapter focuses on the past use of racialized language as one mechanism for evaluating political communication in the 21st century. Specifically, it illuminates this contemporary "caravan crisis" of Central American refugees by locating it within the broader historical pattern of metaphors employed in the construction of U.S. foreign policy toward Latin America.

Chapter 4 - Prayer has traditionally been used in Christianity as a spiritual means to commune with God, but also to beseech God to address the felt needs and fears of the petitioners. But prayer has lately been used in the church by many Nigerian politicians for personal gain. In particular, politicians have deployed prayer as a campaign tool to mobile the church to support the struggle for achieving their political ambitions. In this article the author explores this phenomenon of politicians employing prayer in the church as a potent political tool to subtly campaign for election and reelection in Nigeria. The author would argue that the phenomenon of seeking political power through prayer by politicians confers reciprocal political power on both the politicians and the clergy alike.

In: A Closer Look at Political Communication   ISBN: 978-1-53615-321-7
Editor: Mark H. Tatum   © 2019 Nova Science Publishers, Inc.

Chapter 1

LOCAL PUBLIC SPHERE
AND INFORMATIONAL POLITICS

*Yongjun Shin**

Department of Communication Studies,
Bridgewater State University, Massachusetts, US

ABSTRACT

This study investigates how the local network media help the key
stakeholders to participate in the policy debate regarding a local low-
income housing policy in Madison, Wisconsin, U.S.A., drawing mainly
on Jürgen Habermas's theory of public sphere. Particularly, it aims to
localize Habermas's framework of social structure for local community-
level research. It attempts to demonstrate why and how the rational model
of the public sphere, which relies on rational and consensus-oriented
public discourses, needs to be modified by showing how a contentious
public sphere has emerged in the local network media space. With this
framework and the research findings, it also discusses the media
influence on local community leaders from the perspective of
communication ecology.

* Corresponding Author Email: yongjun.shin@bridgew.edu.

Keywords: local public sphere, informational politics, Jürgen Habermas, communication ecology, network media

INTRODUCTION

Many social researchers argue that emerging electronic media such as the Internet have more potential to work as a public sphere, in which private people come together to articulate and create public opinion with rational-critical debate, than mass media do (Benkler 2006, Castells 2001, Friedland 1996, Gripsrud 2009, Habermas 1992/1996). Like mass media, emerging media also function to allow interactions across different social actors and entities. Yet, the media creates fundamentally different communication spaces by allowing individuals and groups to share information both directly and indirectly and connect with each other in the forms of networks. In other words, it creates a networked public sphere (Ausserhofer and Maireder 2013, Benkler 2006, Friedland, Hove, and Rojas 2006, Habermas 1992/1996).

While there are critiques and warnings about network media space, which can be dominated by cyber-capitalism (Calhoun 1992, 1998, Dean 2002, 2003, 2005, Lyon 2017), it should not be underestimated that network media have granted unprecedented opportunities for the public to share information that was not accessible in the mass media age and to organize themselves for collective action (Benkler 2006, Castells 2001, Friedland 1996). With their open nature, network media both complement and challenge mass media's communication space. In particular, the Internet has fundamentally changed the ways and the goals of engaging in politics and civic engagement, while it cannot substitute for social change or political reform (Castells 2001).

In this vein, this study attempts to assesses how the local network media help some core stakeholders to participate in the policy debate about a local low-income housing policy, drawing mainly on Jürgen Habermas's theory of public sphere. Hence, this research aims to localize Habermas's framework of social structure for local community-level research.

Particularly, the notion of local public sphere is reviewed to discuss the local network media space's role in local public discourses. It also attempts to demonstrate why and how the rational model of public sphere, which relies on rational and consensus-oriented public discourses, needs to be modified by showing how a contentious public sphere has emerged in the local network media space. In this framework, it discusses the media influence on society, particularly policy formation, from the perspective of communication ecology. While the local public sphere is created by the combination of the mass media, the network media, and interpersonal communication spaces, this study focuses on how a part of the network media space, which has been created by some key local stakeholders, challenges the local mass media space. Eventually, it emphasizes that the media influence on policy formation is ecological and interactive among the media institutions and the stakeholders.

LOCALIZING PUBLIC SPHERE

The potential of local network media to enhance local public discourses should be addressed with Habermas's concept of public sphere because Habermas (1992/1996) claims that the development of network media enables communication networks of information and opinions to transform into a public sphere. While Habermas (1962/1989) was critical about mass media institutions earlier, in his book *The Structural Transformation of the Public Sphere*, because they often function as means of propaganda for political power and marketing strategy for corporations, he has shown an enthusiasm for the potential of informational technologies to serve the public sphere in *Between Facts and Norms* (Habermas 1992/1996). He has found that the unfettered circulation of information and opinions through network media contributes to enhancing the democratic exchange of ideas (Habermas 1992/1996).

Although the public sphere has frequently been cited and addressed in social sciences, the concept of local public sphere has been devised and applied in two ways in the United States: the local public sphere as networked communicative space and the local community mass media as a local public sphere. The networked conception of local public sphere has particularly focused on public discourse networks among citizens via internet-based communication such social media as blogs (Friedland et al. 2007). On the other hand, the approach to community mass media as local public sphere has conceptualized community media as a small-scale public sphere that can offer more opportunities to participate in public affairs and access to the media, compared with national media (Stiegler 2009). Along with these frameworks, this research is expected to contribute to the research on local public sphere with a focus on contentious aspect of public discourse. In order to localize Habermas's concept of public sphere to apply to local community-level research, we need to understand how public sphere operates in local communities; this begins with a discussion of Habermas's theory of communicative action, because public sphere is a significant part of the theory.

Habermas's theory of communicative action is briefly defined as action operated by and towards mutual agreement. Since communicative action embraces other communication performances, such as instrumental or strategic self-interested communication, functional regulative communication, symbolic interaction, and others, it lays the overarching foundation for all communication performances (Habermas 1981/1987). In other words, communicative action works as the fundamental ground on which other modes of communication are made possible, and also serves as the medium of socialization, the formation of personalities, and the "competences that make a subject capable of speaking and acting, that put him in a position to take part in processes of reaching understanding and thereby to assert his own identity" (Habermas 1981/1987, 138).

Indeed, Habermas (1981/1987) has developed the concept of communicative action in order to compare the steering media in the dichotomous societal domains of *lifeworld* and *system*. Lifeworld is a universal background composed of language and culture and embedded in personality, society, and culture over time in a variety of social groups, from families to communities. In contrast, system is another societal domain functioning by means-end rationality in the market and the polity.

In Habermas's two-level construction of the world, lifeworld refers to a social realm or sphere of lived experience and social integration, through which social members and institutions are integrated (Habermas 1981/1987). In contrast, system encompasses such aspects of society as the economy and polity that are self-regulating and in which integration takes place through money and power, rather than communication (Habermas 1981/1987).

However, there exists a significant tension between lifeworld and system. That is, even if the subsystems of markets and politics are largely detached from the values and norms of the lifeworld, they still have to rely on it for their reproduction (Habermas 1981/1987). In other words, as long as markets and politics are self-regulating without crisis, they can remain relatively disconnected; however, once the system confronts crisis, it counts on social integration through norms, values, and culture in the lifeworld to provide the reserves for legitimacy, strategic problem solving, and even transformation (Friedland 2001). Furthermore, as the system depends on the resources from the lifeworld, it concomitantly penetrates into and reorganizes the lifeworld through intended and unintended consequences of the economic and political subsystems by instilling their operating logic of power and money into it. As a result, civil society and community life are disrupted, and participatory democratic practices and civic engagement diminish.

In this dynamic, public sphere is located between lifeworld and system by mediating the two social realms with one another. However, the area of public sphere is distinct from the sub-systems because it is basically a site for creating and circulating critical discourses about the systems. Nevertheless, it plays a crucial integrating role for societies by enabling the systems to be sensitive about the public opinions generated from lifeworld (Habermas 1981/1987). On the other hand, it offers the public the opportunity to check the systems through their critical discourses and collective actions (Habermas 1981/1987). For this, Habermas (1962/1989) pays particular attention to the eighteenth century's bourgeois public sphere, in which the participants used reason in rational-critical debate, and which functioned to check domination by the state and illegitimate use of power. For instance, Habermas interprets Britain's coffee houses, France's salons, and Germany's Tischgesellschaften as the bourgeois public sphere, where public issues were shared and discussed among all classes of citizens (Habermas 1962/1989).

Hence, as we localize Habermas's framework of social structure to understand local community structure, it enables us to identify a local public sphere operating between local lifeworld and local systems of polity and economy. Therefore, this study conceptualizes that the congregation of local lifeworlds constitutes a local community. Local public sphere is composed of diverse communication spaces from local mass media, network media, and non-mediated forms of public discourse. An advantage of this conceptualization might be that this localized framework of social structure can contribute to overcoming the controversial idea of Habermas's universal norms and values through communicative action among competent speakers. That is to say, while Habermas's universal validity claims are more likely to be discussed by universal participants at the level of the lifeworld, in contrast, at a community level, community members—a particular group of people—are more likely to reach understanding and agreement on ethical claims through communicative action than on universal validity claims, because they discursively engage in more limited *ethical claims* (Habermas 1992/1996). For instance, local low-income housing policy issues are often discussed by local community members with such ethical claims as local economic integration and residential diversity.

In sum, through localizing Habermas's framework of social structure for local community studies, we can identify that a local community consists of different social domains that have different principles of transaction and interaction. At least three large social realms can be identified in a local community: the local polity, local economy, and ordinary citizens' lifeworld. In addition, local media are also conceptualized to possess the potential to operate as local public sphere in which local community members discuss local issues and reach an agreement through critical-rational discourses. This research, particularly, focuses on how the local network media space has worked as a local public sphere regarding the focal policy issue. However, as addressed below, the model of public sphere, which is conceptualized to be the site of rational and consensus-oriented public deliberation, confronts challenges from the counterargument of a contentious public deliberation process and the nature of network media spaces, which allow unfiltered interactions. Therefore, a modified model of public sphere is addressed below, which includes contentious and irrational public discourses.

INFORMATIONAL POLITICS AND CONTENTIONS PUBLIC SPHERE

Public policy-making process is the most popular legislative and administrative action in democratic society. People tend to think that such process might take place through formal directions and very orderly, rational discursive procedures. However, public policy making is a most contentious, complex, and dynamic process, which engages a variety of actors, issues, actions, and stages. The policy-making process is a struggle per se where events do not proceed neatly in stages, steps, or phases; instead, independent streams that flow through the system all at once, each with a life of its own and equal with one another, become coupled when a policy window opens (Kingdon 1995, Mettler and Soss 2004). Series of events also engage in a struggle among parties with different viewpoints and interests, and struggles take place in several discursive platforms (Young 2000, Cohen and Fung 2004, Scholz 2017). Therefore, from a deliberative aspect of democratic practice, democracy is not only a means through which citizens can maximize their interests and check the power of rulers, but also a means of collective problem solving that depends on the expression and criticism of the diverse opinions of all the members of the society for its legitimacy and wisdom (Young 2000, May 2013, Dryzek 2006).

However, some formulations of ideals of deliberative democracy tend to restrict their conception of political communication to argument, and to

have a too biased or narrow understanding of what being reasonable means
(Young 2000, 2001, Healy 2011). To the extent that norms of deliberation
implicitly value certain styles of expression as dispassionate, orderly, or
articulate, they can have exclusivity implications by dismissing the
important role other forms of communication play in furthering inclusive
democratic outcomes (Young 2000, 2001). Particularly, under
circumstances where there are serious conflicts that arise from structural
positions of privilege and disadvantage, and/or where subordinated, less
powerful, or minority groups find their interests ignored in public debate,
disorderliness is an important tool of critical communication aimed at
calling attention to the unreasonableness of others (Young 2000, May
2013). Therefore, in a society where there are social group differences and
significant injustice, democratic politics ought to be a process of struggle;
struggle is a process of communicative engagement of citizens with one
another (Young 2000, May 2013, Dryzek 2006).

In sum, the public sphere model, which is based on rational and
consensus-oriented public discourse, is challenged by the question of
irrational struggles in the uneven power structure. When we set up too-
rigorous measures of the public deliberation process in the public sphere,
significant voices and issues can be underestimated and dismissed. As
Habermas (1992/1996) implies with his later idea of networked public
sphere, the model of public sphere should seriously take plurality into
account. The plurality should be embraced in terms of issue, participant,
and mode of public discourse as well. This research particularly concerns
the mode of public deliberation, because contentious, irrational mode of
public discourse is a significant aspect of public deliberation in the public
sphere.

In contemporary societies, technological innovation tends to facilitate
contentious and irrational modes of public discourses in cyberspace. The
development of information and communication technologies enables
network media spaces to become "a global electronic agora where the
diversity of human disaffection explodes in a cacophony of accents"
(Castells 2001, 138). For instance, because network media spaces are open

to everyone, there are innumerable unreliable rumors and conspiracy theories that flow on Internet websites (Castells 2001, Benkler 2006).

While many such unfiltered contents are produced and circulated in network media spaces, the media spaces play an important role in "informational politics," in which heretical politicians, uncommon journalists, social activists, and active ordinary citizens disseminate political information and news through network media spaces (Castells 1997, 310-311). Such informational politics is distinguished from the politics fostered by mass media because the mass media-leading politics operate mainly based on the images and the scandals of political actors that are portrayed by mass media (Rose–Ackerman 1999, Castells 2001, Thompson 2000). Some outcomes of informational politics are described as follows:

The borderline between gossip, fantasy, and valuable political information becomes increasingly blurred, thus further complicating the use of information as the privileged political weapon in the Internet Age. Therefore, for the time being, rather than strengthening democracy by fostering the knowledge and participation of the citizens, use of the Internet tends to deepen the crisis of political legitimacy by providing a broader launching platform for the politics of scandal (Castells 2001, 158).

Therefore, network media spaces come to be filled with rational and irrational, and consensual and contentious modes of public discourse, which eventually make the public become plural and reorganized in the form of networks according to issues, values, and interests. In short, such fragmented networks of the public eventually create networked public spheres through network media (Benkler 2006, Friedland, Hove, and Rojas 2006, Habermas 1992/1996).

Therefore, network media spaces should not be conceived as generating only a rational, consensus-oriented model of public sphere. Such a rationalist model of public sphere prevents Habermas's theory of public sphere from evolving into an inclusive and pluralist model of public sphere by excluding or degrading irrational, contentious modes of public discourses, which might be employed by those who are powerless but have legitimate claims. Indeed, network media spaces are sites of conflicting networks; hence, the conflicting and contested aspect of the media spaces should inevitably be taken into account (Dean 2002, 2003). Therefore, this research insists that a contentious model of public sphere works better to represent the real public deliberation phenomena in network media spaces than rational, consensus-oriented models do.

In short, by *localizing* Habermas's concept of public sphere to apply to meso-level community research, this research investigates the local public sphere, where some key local stakeholders have participated in the policy debate about Madison's local low-income housing policy of inclusionary zoning. While the policy case of Madison took place about a decade ago, it deem still valid and useful because there has not been much change in the communication media environment for public discourses such as policy debate where such social media as blogs are widely and frequently used. Hence, by reviewing the public discourses in the local network media spaces regarding a local low-income housing policy in Madison, this research attempts to investigate a contentious mode of public discourse in a modeling of local public sphere.

INFORMATIONAL POLITICS ON MADISON'S LOW-INCOME HOUSING POLICY

A mid-sized U.S. city, Madison, Wisconsin, legislated inclusionary zoning, a local ordinance, which demands or supports housing developers to offer a certain percentage of new housings to low-income households in 2004. The ordinance was initiated by a new progressive mayor and crated by progressive city politicians. However, due to the strong oppositions from local stakeholders, particularly conservative politicians and local construction businesses, the law had to be expired in 2009 without making a significant contribution to local affordable housing issue.

In terms of research methods, this research has employed various web search engines with the subjects of "Madison's inclusionary zoning" and "affordable housing." It has also checked all the web- sites of local construction companies and the civic organizations that have been identified through reviewing public documents and the local newspapers' coverage of the issue.

Through the data gathering process, this research has found that two city alders' blogs have played significant roles in participating in the policy debate, while it has not found any other stakeholders or organizations that used network media to participate in the policy debate. In addition, this research has identified a local online publication web- site, Dane101, which has produced some articles about IZ. On the site, one alder, as a contributing writer, has participated in the policy debate. A local citizen journalism project, Madison Commons, has provided the local newspapers' news articles about the issue, without producing its own news stories. Therefore, its coverage has not been analyzed.

In addition, three core stakeholders were interviewed: a city alder, a housing developer, and an urban planner. While the two alders have employed the blogs during the most critical period for IZ debate, when the enacted IZ ordinance was challenged by a local developers' association and a local apartment owners' association, only one alder, was available for the interview.

A progressive city alder, who actually worked as the main policy-maker, ran three blogs to address local affordable housing issues: *In Search of Inclusionary Zoning* (afterward *In Search of IZ*), and *Affordable Housing Alliance* (afterward *AHA*). She has written articles about IZ on *In Search of IZ* and her personal blog while using *AHA* to address general affordable housing issues. In addition, she, as a guest writer, has posted a few articles about IZ on *Dane101*. On the other hand, a conservative city alder, who was the main opponent of the progressive alder, used his blog *Upstreaming* to express his opinions about Madison's inclusionary zoning in a relatively small amount of posts. The two alders intensively and strategically used the blog media to participate in the policy debate.

The progressive alder has played multiple roles in the local politics as an alder, the director of a nonprofit organization, and a member of a progressive political party, while running the three blogs. Through the network media, she has presented detailed information about the equity model for IZ-unit buyers, incentives for developers, IZ waivers, and IZ-unit marketing. Also, she has tried to publicize the city politics, which took place even in some informal meetings among various stakeholders such as local developers, realtors, and politicians. On *In Search for IZ*, she described:

> Last Thursday (June 29) the Mayor's workgroup had a very sparcely attended meeting (Jed Sanborn, Golden, Palm, myself and the Mayor) and we approved the final report. (You might be wondering which alders have not yet been mentioned, those would be Bruer, Rosas, Cnare, Knox and Radomski, and while Cnare sits on the Plan Commission, the rest have hardly been heard from.) There is much going on before the special council meeting on July 11th on Inclusionary Zoning. On Thursday, July 6th, the Plan Commission will have its final meeting and make its final proposals. On Monday, July 10th at noon, the Common Council will be having a special brown bag lunch to discuss Inclusionary Zoning and on July 11th, hopefully, we will vote on something.

In addition, she has actively monitored the local mass media's coverage and other stakeholders' political discourses in the network media space and responded to the discourses. For instance, on her blogs, she reacted to *WSJ*'s coverage of the policy issue:

> Too bad the Wisconsin State Journal can't also at least try to be gracious as well. And that the Realtors didn't send them the same message. I was a little surprised to read the Scott Milfred column (he's the editor of the editorial page) in yesterday's paper. Unfortunately, he's still spouting incorrect information likely given to him by the Realtors.

In addition, she reacted to the conservative alder's posting:

> Zach Brandon is working hard to convince readers of his blog that Madison doesn't need Inclusionary Zoning because there is plenty of affordable housing available. Of course, anyone who has tried to rent or buy a home in Madison knows just how hard it is to find affordable housing.

She has also acted like a citizen journalist when covering the issue by trying to debunk the myths of the fear about IZ's adverse effects by providing factual knowledge that can prove the groundlessness of the anti-IZ attacks. She even visited to check the construction site and criticized the developers' reluctance to implement the law while she has tried to reveal the stories that were not covered by the mass media.

On the other hand, the conservative has used his blog *Upstreaming* to express his opinions about Madison's inclusionary zoning with a relatively small amount of posts. He tried to advocate for developers' interests by expressing his concern about 100% cost offsets for IZ-participating developers, based on the fairness of the law. For instance, he said:

> At a recent IZ workgroup meeting, I asked a very simple question based on David Rus''s Nine Lessons for Inclusionary Zoning: As a *statement of principle*, do you believe that the cost of Inclusionary Zoning should be 100% offset by the incentives? The reason this is important is because if you don't, the costs of the subsidy will be shifted to the other 85% of the homebuyers. Put more simply... It will make housing more expensive!

He has also emphasized the unconstitutionality of IZ, as was ruled in San Diego, and the fact that Madison has enough affordable housing. Moreover, he has attacked the progressive alder for her intransigence for keeping IZ. On his blog, Brandon criticizes:

> After this petty maneuver, this same alder wrote this in a post today: ... the bottom line is that I wanted an ordinance that was going to work and I don't care about what silly political games people want to play ...

And, just before the vote this alder wrote: Too bad some people are too busy spinning and trying to score political points, instead of trying to be constructive and help create affordable housing for our community... I'd rather stay focused on bettering our community and doing my job as an alder . . . and wake up tomorrow morning with a clear conscience and pride in my integrity. There is nothing worse than a hypocrite who thinks they are a martyr. Get off the cross, Brenda... we are going to need the wood to build affordable housing.

In sum, while the progressive local politician was considered a maverick alder, the conservative alder was self-identified as a centrist who opposes both extreme right and left wings in terms of political ideology. The two city politicians have been at odds with each other regarding the IZ issue. However, the struggles were not merely between the two politicians; they have intended to influence the local politics, and many local elites and citizens referred to the public discourses from the local network media space. For instance, the progressive alder (personal communication, 3 March 2009) maintained:

> I would say a lot of city staff read it. And, I think a lot of younger people read it. And, people who are political active read it. Like a lot of people tell me that, it is the only place to find local news. So, there is a council meeting tonight. I will write everything that happens in the council meeting and print out on the blog. So, if you are interested in local politics, you want to know what is going on, they tell me that it is the only place to find out. So, the city staff would read it. Anybody who is following any issue that is sort of local will read it.

Indeed, while interviewing with several key stakeholders, this research has also found that most of them monitored some key local figures' blogs, including two politicians. From the conservative politician's posting on his blog, this research has also identified that even the mayor monitored the local network media space and reacted to the contents.

SEMANTIC NETWORKS ON MADISON'S IZ

In the informational politics, this research has identified total fifteen distinctive semantic themes on the blogs as shown in Table 1. This research identifies and selects themes in a qualitative way by: 1) reading every blog posting that has covered inclusionary zoning and relevant issues; 2) extracting the arguments and statements, which indicate and imply the stakeholders' standpoints toward the IZ issue and the political opponent; 3) selecting significantly distinctive meanings and ideas as themes; 4) enumerating all repeated meanings and ideas; and 5) deciding the final themes and creating a theme inventory, considering the entire relations among the themes. In order to finalize the theme inventory, the researcher was engaged in thorough discussion with other media researcher to articulate and verify each theme while reading all the postings and updating the theme inventory over time (see Table 1).

Table 1. Themes inventory from network media's coverage

Themes	Meanings based on frame elements
Social remedy	IZ contributes to such social problems as affordable housing crisis, rising housing price, and urban planning.
Social burden	IZ causes unintended and undesired social burden such as tax increase and local school system's budget challenge.
Social benefit	IZ contributes to children's education, community integration, and economic integration.
Anti-free market	Developers should be forced to provide affordable housing.
Pro-free market	Affordable housing should be dealt with by housing market.
Legitimacy	Mandatory IZ enactment is legitimate in terms of timing, efficacy, and legality.
Illegitimacy	Mandatory IZ is illegitimate due to the conflict with upper laws, inefficiency and politics. Voluntary is alternative.
Success	IZ ordinance is successful to achieve its goals.
Illegitimate critique about IZ	Some stakeholders' critiques about IZ is illegitimate.
Progressive politician's hypocrisy	Some progressive politicians' attitudes toward IZ are hypocritical.
Developers' resistance as obstacle	Developers' resistance against IZ is the main obstacle in implementing IZ.
Protection of developers' interests	Developers' interests should be protected in the process of implementing IZ.
Conservative mass media's misleading coverage	Conservative mass media disseminate misleading information about IZ.
Politics as an obstacle to IZ	Conservative politicians exert politics to oppose IZ.

A comparison of theme frequencies shows the differences in the policy debate in the local network media space. The progressive alder's personal blog and *In Search of IZ* has disseminated the themes that supported IZ 87 times. On the contrary, the conservative's *Upstreaming* has been filled with the themes that opposed IZ 7 times. *Dane101* has produced the themes that supported IZ 22 times.

Through the two blogs, the progressive alder has focused on the developers' resistance to comply with the IZ ordinance by most frequently repeating that theme ("developers' resistance as obstacle" theme 25 times). In addition, she has also tried to protect the law by portraying some IZ opponents' critiques as illegitimate ("illegitimate critique about IZ" frame 18 times) and also arguing that the law is legitimate ("legitimacy" theme 10 times). Moreover, she has been skeptical about the private sectors' efforts for affordable housing ("anti-free market" theme 12 times) and has tried to associate conservative politicians' politics with a main obstacle to IZ ("politics as an obstacle to IZ" theme 7 times). She has even pointed out conservative local mass media's misleading coverage as an obstacle to IZ ("conservative mass media's misleading coverage" theme 1 time). In addition, her claims have included IZ as "social benefit" (7 times) and "social remedy" (5 times).

On the other hand, the conservative alder has criticized IZ supporters, particularly the progressive alder, and tried to defend the developers' interest through *Upstreaming*. "Protection of developers' interest" theme has appeared 3 times. IZ has been depicted as an illegitimate method to supply affordable housing ("illegitimacy" theme 2 times). While the conservative politician has argued that affordable housing should be dealt with by the housing market through the "pro-free market" theme, he has portrayed the progressive politician's effort with "progressive politician's hypocrisy" theme.

Dane101 has also supported IZ through various themes. Like *In Search of IZ*, it has also emphasized the developers' resistance to comply with the IZ ordinance through "developers' resistance as obstacle" theme (6 times). In addition, the "anti-free market" (4 times), "progressive ideology" (3 times), "social remedy" (3 times), and "success" (2 times) themes have been used. Furthermore, it has employed the "conservative mass media's misleading coverage" (2 times), "illegitimate critique about IZ" (1 time), and "politics as an obstacle to IZ" (1 time) themes to criticize the IZ opponents.

In sum, the analysis has found that the policy debate in the local network media space has been dominated by IZ-supporting semantic themes. Many IZ-supporting themes were targeted at developers, realtors, and conservative politicians who opposed IZ. On the contrary, the IZ-opposing themes were relatively weak because there was only one blog, operated by the conservative politician, to oppose IZ. Nevertheless, the conservative politician's themes have been quite contemptuous by labeling the opponent with inflammatory theme. For instance, on *Upstreaming*, the conservative politician said:

> Hypocrisy = Beliefs - Actions... There is always a story inside the story when it comes to this council. There are things the public would never hear, but probably should. For months, I have debated whether to put these stories on this Blog. For the record, I am not talking about muckraking or pointing out legislative inconsistencies. I am talking about pointing out full-on hypocrisy: "the act of pretending to have virtues that one does not truly possess or practice."

The progressive politician has not also participated in the debate only with factual and rational discourses all the time. She has also employed aggressive, contentious discourses. For instance, on her personal blog, she said:

> My guess is that if someone put together a serious proposal, I'd vote for it if it makes sense. If I put together a proposal, 8 people would automatically vote against it because it is my idea and I'd be labeled a communist or spendthrift.

In addition, when the progressive criticized the leader of a local realtors association, she posted her comment on her personal blog as follows:

How arrogant can someone be that they think that they get a special process and have to be consulted before things get done? I guess, these are the special favors lobbyists expect, I'm just not used to them demanding them so publicly. They sure have gotten brazen since they were able to gut the lobbying ordinance and they've gotten all the media support for their anti-business rhetoric.

In short, such unfiltered discourses have not been rare in the policy debates in the local network media space. Therefore, a contentious local public sphere has emerged in the local network media space, where some stakeholders have participated in the policy debate with not only critical and rational, but also contentious, irrational public discourses. Moreover, this research has found that one of the main motivations why the city politicians utilized blogs to participate in the policy debate was their dissatisfaction with the local media's coverage of the issue. This finding leads us to address the mass media's influence on local communities, especially on local community leaders.

LOCAL MASS MEDIA'S INFLUENCE ON COMMUNITY LEADERS

This study has also identified that many key stakeholders have participated in the policy formation process with preconceived opinions and attitudes toward the issue. For instance, the progressive politician answered the question about media influence on her idea:

I focus more on what is right than what media is going to say. I don't usually write press releases, and sometimes because the media is sort of not covering things. They don't even cover it. So, it doesn't even matter what they think (personal communication, B. Konkel, 3 March 2009).

In addition, even the network media has not seemed to affect the stakeholders' perceptions and understandings of the issue to a great extent. Some key stakeholders have acknowledged that they just keep checking and monitoring other key stakeholders' blogs and web-sites because they merely want to know how other stakeholders think. For instance, a local residential building developer (personal communication, J. Rosenberg, 22 May 2009) said that he judges and acts for local issues based on the facts his team gathers even though he reads almost every local newspaper and some key stakeholders' network media including the progressive alder's blog, the mayor's, and others. Also, a member of Madison's Inclusionary Zoning Advisory Committee said about his blog reading:

> I read as many as alders' blogs and currents. Brenda Konkel is very good at everyday writing. I read mayor's [blog]. I read Kristian's [blog] at *Cap Times*. It is interesting secondary news source. It gives me a little more insight of individual people. It helps me know the writers. I am not trying to pay enough attention to anonymous stuff. Taken as a whole, it is really an opportunity to understand thought processes to some degree (B. Munson, personal communication, 21 May 2009).

Therefore, this research has found that some key stakeholders' perceptions didn't seem to be influenced by media coverage, although this study could not examine all the stakeholders' media readerships. So, we can raise an important question: why do the stakeholders keep writing their ideas and thoughts about the local issues and checking other media's contents? Responding to this critical question, this research speculates that stakeholders write articles and monitor one another's contents on the network media 1) because they want to affect the public's perception of certain issues, so as to obtain public legitimacy for their own ideas and standpoints, and 2) because they are concerned about whether the public is influenced by other media. In short, the driving force for stakeholders to use network media to engage in symbolic struggle for certain social issues is the perception of the stakeholders that the public's perception is sensitive or susceptible to the media's coverage, regardless of whether or how many ordinary citizens read them.

Nevertheless, this study does not insist that media do not affect the public's perception. As many media-effect studies have still shown, media indeed influence and change humans' perceptions, so that they sometimes contribute to changing societies. However, what this research attempts to demonstrate is that studies of media's influence on our society should be diversified. As this case study of a local policy issue shows, at least the media's influence on community leaders can be ecological and interactive among stakeholders and media entities.

CONCLUSION

This research has assessed how the local network media helped some key stakeholders participate in the policy debate through a case study of a local low-income housing policy. The online contentious public sphere has enabled key stakeholders to lead informational politics, with which they could disseminate the information about the local politics to the public in order to gain public legitimacy for their standpoints. Through the analyses of the public discourses in the local network media space, this research has found that the network media has served as the communication space for not only rational, critical debates, but also irrational, contentious communicative struggles where the public discourses have often been disturbed and divided. Consequently, it came up with a model of contentious local public sphere, a conceptualization based on the localization of Habermas's framework of social structure, including public sphere, and a critical review of rational models of public sphere and technological innovation.

In addition, this research has observed that the boundary between local politics and civic engagement has become blurred particularly in the case of the progressive local politician who has engaged in city politics and civic activism, and tried to bridge the two realms, as described in Castells's (2001) informational politics. As demonstrated in her work, the progressive politician played multiple roles as a local politician, a nonprofit organization leader, and an activist. In her informational politics, she has brought her agendas rooted in local activism and community engagement to the city governance and politics.

When it comes to the local mass media's influence on community leaders, this study attempts to draw on communication ecology. The ecological media research responds to contemporary social transformations toward network society and applies network and ecological perspectives of social studies for media research (Friedland 2001, Ball-Rokeach, Kim, and Matei 2001). In this framework, communication media need to be understood in their interactions with one another and other social institutions. For this reason, we need to add more complexity and dynamics to media research models by considering the interactive influences among media entities, and other social agents and entities. Particularly, emerging network media increase the dynamics of public discourses in traditional mass media and network media spaces. Therefore, the influence of media on social issues also needs to be investigated in an ecological and interactive framework.

While this study has investigated core local community leaders' informational politics, this study has left some limitations. Most of all, it couldn't assess the mayor's informational politics due to his limited visibility on the local network space and availability for the research. Since he put forth the policy from the beginning of his term, it might have provided more intriguing findings in the local informational politics with his active engagement in it. Also, further research can be envisioned to investigate the influence of local community leaders' informational politics on community members in the framework of communication ecology since citizens are also a significant stakeholder group in the network of local politics, which affect community issues.

ACKNOWLEDGMENTS

The author is very grateful for the guidance and encouragement received from Dr. Lewis A. Friedland in the School of Journalism and Mass Communication at the University of Wisconsin–Madison.

FUNDING

This project is supported by the U.S. Department of Housing and Urban Development under the *Doctoral Dissertation Research Grant* (H-21538SG); and both the International Communication Association and the Urban Communication Foundation under the *James Carey Urban Communication Award*.

REFERENCES

Ausserhofer, Julian, and Axel Maireder. 2013. "National politics on Twitter: Structures and topics of a networked public sphere." *Information, Communication & Society* 16 (3):291-314.

Ball-Rokeach, Sandra J., Yong-Chan Kim, and Sorin Matei. 2001. "Storytelling neighborhood: Paths to belonging in diverse urban environments." *Communication Research* 28 (4):392-428.

Benkler, Yochai. 2006. *The wealth of networks: How social production transforms markets and freedom.* New Haven, CT: Yale University Press.

Calhoun, Craig. 1992. "The infrastructure of modernity: Indirect social relationships, information technology, and social integration." In *Social Change and Modernity*, edited by N. Smelser and H. Haferkamp, 205-236. Berkeley, CA: University of California Press.

Calhoun, Craig. 1998. "Community without propinquity revisited: Communications technology and the transformation of the urban public sphere." *Sociological Inquiry* 68 (3):373-397. doi: 10.1111/j.1475-682X.1998.tb00474.x.

Castells, Manuel 1997. *The power of identity.* Oxford: Blackwell Publishers.

Castells, Manuel 2001. *The internet galaxy: Reflections on the Internet, business, and society.* New York: Oxford University Press.

Cohen, Joshua, and Archon Fung. 2004. "Radical democracy." *Swiss journal of political science* 10 (4):23-34.

Dean, Jodi. 2002. *Publicity's secret: How technoculture capitalizes on democracy*. Ithaca, NY: Cornell University Press.

Dean, Jodi. 2003. "Why the net is not a public sphere." *Constellations* 10 (1):95-112.

Dean, Jodi. 2005. "Communicative capitalism: Circulation and the foreclosure of politics." *Cultural Politics* 1 (1):51-74.

Dryzek, John S. 2006. *Deliberative global politics: Discourse and democracy in a divided world*. Cambridge: Polity.

Friedland, Lewis A., Tom Hove, and Hernando Rojas. 2006. "The networked public sphere." *Javnost-the Public* 13 (4):5-26.

Friedland, Lewis A. 1996. "Electronic democracy and the new citizenship." *Media, Culture & Society* 18 (2):185-212.

Friedland, Lewis A. 2001. "Communication, community, and democracy: Toward a theory of the communicatively integrated community." *Communication Research* 28 (4):358-391.

Friedland, Lewis A., Chris Long, Yongjun Shin, and Nakho Kim. 2007. "The local publc sphere as a networked space." In *Media and public sphere*, edited by Richard Butsch, 43-57. New York: Palgrave Macmillan.

Gripsrud, Jostein. 2009. "Digitising the public sphere: Two key issues." *Javnost-The Public* 16 (1):5-16.

Habermas, Jürgen. 1981/1987. *The theory of communicative action: Lifeworld and system: A critique of functionalist reason*. Translated by T. McCarthy. Vol. 2. Boston: Beacon Press.

Habermas, Jürgen. 1992/1996. *Between facts and norms: Contributions to a discourse theory of law and democracy*. Translated by W. Rehg. Cambridge, MA: MIT Press

Habermas, Jürgen. 1962/1989. *The structural transformation of the public sphere*. Translated by T. Burger. Cambridge, MA: MIT Press.

Healy, Paul. 2011. "Rethinking deliberative democracy: From deliberative discourse to transformative dialogue." *Philosophy & Social Criticism* 37 (3):295-311.

Kingdon, John W. 1995. *Agendas, alternatives, and public policies*. 2 ed. New York: Haper Collins College Publishers.

Lyon, David. 2017. "Digital Citizenship and Surveillance| Surveillance Culture: Engagement, Exposure, and Ethics in Digital Modernity." *International Journal of Communication* 11:19.

May, Stephen. 2013. *Language and minority rights: Ethnicity, nationalism and the politics of language*. New York: Routledge.

Mettler, Suzanne, and Joe Soss. 2004. "The consequences of public policy for democratic citizenship: Bridging policy studies and mass politics." *Perspectives on politics* 2 (1):55-73.

Rose–Ackerman, Susan. 1999. *Corruption and government*. Cambridge: Cambridge University Press.

Scholz, Sally J. 2017. "Iris Marion Young on responsible intervention: reimagining humanitarian intervention." *Journal of Global Ethics* 13 (1):70-89.

Stiegler, Zack. 2009. "Conceptualising the small-scale public sphere." *Javnost-The Public* 16 (2):41-59. doi: 10.1080/13183222.2009. 11009003.

Thompson, John B. 2000. *Political scandal: Power and visibility in the media age*. Cambridge: Polity Press.

Young, Iris Marion. 2000. *Inclusion and democracy*. New York: Oxford University Press.

Young, Iris Marion. 2001. "Activist challenges to deliberative democracy." *Political theory* 29 (5):670-690.

BIOGRAPHICAL SKETCH

Yongjun Shin

Affiliation: Department of Communication Studies, Bridgewater State University, MA, USA

Education:
- 2009 PhD Mass Communication, University of Wisconsin-Madison
- 2004 MA Communication-Urban Studies, Michigan State University
- 1999 BA Journalism, Sungkyunkwan University, Seoul, S. Korea

Research and Professional Experience:
- 2018 - present, Assessing senses of place in the brain: Neuroscientific implications for public place-making with an external research grant preparation, collaboration with Dr. Gary Gumpert in the Urban Communication Foundation and Dr. Susan Drucker in the School of Communication, Hofstra University
- 2018 - present, Building culturally integrated communities: Relational and reflexive approach to racial and ethnic biases intervention with an external research grant preparation
- 2018 - present, Community resources and communications mapping project with an external research grant preparation, Bridgewater State University
- 2016 - 2018, Interdisciplinary racial and ethnic biases intervention program project, collaboration with Dr. Ahmed M. Abdelal in the Department of Communication Sciences and Disorders, Bridgewater State University
- 2014 - 2015, Community development project for Bridgewater downtown redevelopment, Bridgewater State University and Town of Bridgewater
- 2014 - 2015, Community development project for Bridgewater town identity building, Bridgewater State University and Town of Bridgewater
- 2011 - 2012, Survey Research for Korean Catholic Community of Boston, Survey Research Committee, Korean Catholic Community of Boston

- 2010 - 2011, Social media and privacy, Fixed-Term Research Assistant Professor, Department of Interaction Science, Sungkyunkwan University, Seoul
- 2009 - 2010, Community informatics and new urbanism, Postdoctoral research fellow co-worked with Professor Dong Hee Shin, Department of Interaction Science, Sungkyunkwan University, Seoul
- 2007 - 2008, Analysis of Canadian Digital Content Initiatives and Digitization Projects, Researcher by contract with the Korea Information Technology Industry Promotion Agency
- 2007 - 2008, Analysis of U.S. Cable Television Programming and Content Development, Researcher by contract with the Korea Digital Cable Laboratories
- 2006 - 2007, Citizen Journalism Project, Researcher co-worked with Dr. Lewis Friedland, Center for Communication and Democracy, School of Journalism and Mass Communication, and Dr. Hernando Rojas, Department of Life Science Communication, University of Wisconsin-Madison
- 2005 - 2006, Madison Metropolitan School District Project, Researcher co-worked with Dr. Lewis Friedland, Center for Communication and Democracy School of Journalism and Mass Communication, University of Wisconsin-Madison
- 2005 - 2006, Model Communities, Pathway to Independence, federally funded by Medicaid Infrastructure Grant Program; Department of Family and Health Service, State of Wisconsin, Project Assistant under the supervision of Policy Analyst Molly Michels, Waisman Center, University of Wisconsin-Madison
- 2004 - 2006, Assistive Technology Maintenance and Repair Project Pathway to Independence, federally funded by Medicaid Infrastructure Grant Program, Department of Family and Health Service, State of Wisconsin, Project Assistant under the supervision of Dr. Jay K. Martin, Mechanical Engineering, University of Wisconsin-Madison

- 2004 - 2005, Media-Violence Abstracts and Database: A Web-Based Resource funded by the Center for Successful Parenting, Research Assistant under the supervision of Dr. Joanne Cantor, Communication Arts, University of Wisconsin-Madison
- 2004, Community Health and Social Capital; Center for Urban Affairs Michigan State University. Research Assistant for Dr. John Schweitzer
- 2003, Capital City Airport Survey; Department of Communication Michigan State University. Research Assistant for Department Chair Dr. Charles Atkin
- 2003, 17th Annual Neighborhood Association Meeting Evaluation, MI; Center for Urban Affairs, Michigan State University. Research Assistant for Dr. John Schweitzer
- 2003, Social Capital in Tri-Counties, MI; Urban Affairs Programs Michigan State University. Research Assistant for Dr. John Schweitzer
- 2003 - 2004, Sense of Community in Lansing Neighborhood Project; Urban Affairs Programs, Michigan State University. Research Assistant for Dr. John Schweitzer
- 2003, Coolkid Choices Program: Increasing Attention Competency through Preschool Children's Delay of Gratification; Urban Affairs Programs, Michigan State University. Research Assistant in preparing research grant proposal to U.S. Department of Health and Human Services for Acting Dean Dr. Dozier Thronton and Dr. Robert Griffore
- 2002 - 2003, Anti-Predatory Lending Project; Urban Affairs Programs Michigan State University. Research Assistant for Dr. Joe Darden

Professional Appointments:
- 2017 – present Bridgewater State University, Associate Professor

- 2017 – 2017   University of California, San Diego, Visiting Scholar
- 2014 – 2014   Sungkyunkwan University, Invited Visiting Professor
- 2011 – 2017   Bridgewater State University, Assistant Professor
- 2010 – 2011   Bridgewater State University, Visiting Lecturer
- 2009 – 2010   Sungkyunkwan University, Postdoctoral Fellow
- 2007 – 2009   University of Wisconsin-Madison, Fellow

Honors:
- Sabbatical leave, fall semester 2017
- Academic Excellence Award & May Celebration Honoree, Bridgewater State University, 2012 - 2018
- James W. Carey Urban Communication Award *inaugural recipient, International Communication Association, 2008
- Top Student Paper Award, Philosophy of Communication Division, International Communication Association, 2008
- Fellowship, School of Journalism and Mass Communication, University of Wisconsin-Madison, 2007 - 2009
- Graduate Research Award, School of Journalism and Mass Communication, University of Wisconsin-Madison, 2008
- Vilas Travel Fellowship, Graduate School, University of Wisconsin-Madison, 2007 & 2008
- Undergraduate Academic Excellence Scholarship, Sungkyunkwan University, Seoul, 1998

Publications from the Last 3 Years:
- Shin, Y., Park, H. S., Han, S. S., & Chang, W. (2018). Information seeking tactics and sense of workplace community in Korea. *Journal of Community Psychology, 46*(7), 856-870. Published online before print, March, 31, 2018, doi: 10.1002/jcop.21977
- Shin, Y., & Shin, D. H. (2017). Modeling community resources and communications mapping for strategic inter-organizational

problem solving and civic engagement. *Journal of Urban Technology*, *23*(4), 47-66. Published online before print, February, 13, 2017, doi:10.1080/10630732.2016.1175826

- Shin, Y. (2016). Connecting political communication with urban politics: A Bourdieusian framework. *International Journal of Communication*, *10*, 508-529.

In: A Closer Look at Political Communication   ISBN: 978-1-53615-321-7
Editor: Mark H. Tatum   © 2019 Nova Science Publishers, Inc.

Chapter 2

NEIGHBORHOOD EFFECT AND *MILLET KIRAATHANE* AS A SPACE FOR POLITICAL COMMUNICATION

Recep Gulmez[*]*, PhD*

Department of Political Science and Public Administration
Erzincan Binali Yildirim University, Erzincan, Turkey

ABSTRACT

Coffee-houses (*Kahvehane*) and Public Reading Houses *(Kıraathane)* are two public places where people enjoy their free time sipping their teas or coffees and talk about politics. In the Turkish society, since 1500s, during the reign of the Ottoman Empire, these two places have been spaces where politics is intensively discussed, decision is given for the selection of political power and where the government is criticized. In addition to being public reading house, the *Kıraathane* can be defined as a place where people have been enlightened from the past to the present, the political power is criticized where urban and rural life are united while drinking coffee and tea. These public reading houses are spaces open to the public in the ottoman empire during the reign of

[*] Corresponding Author Email: rgulmez@erzincan.edu.tr.

Suleyman the Magnificent, where the authority was thought to be weakened by means of the rumors in these places. On the other hand, the coffee-house is a place where the local people taste their coffee originally from Yemen and discuss how to overthrow the political power, discuss daily problems and make philosophical debates. During the Ottoman Empire, coffee houses were very often shut down in case riots could arise among the people by giving the excuse that coffee was not good for health and should be forbidden for religious reasons. Coffee-houses and public reading houses are places today where political communication is often established, and the neighborhood effect is most often felt. It can be described not only as tea-coffee drinking places where free time is passed, but also as places where voter behavior begins to form and democracy is created. In one study on coffee-houses, it is mentioned that in the 1960s there were not coffeehouses in the southeastern Anatolia in Turkey since the sheiks or leaders of the clans in the region did not want any opposition to their authority and rule. Based on this example, it is clear that the coffee-houses and public reading houses are spaces for political communication and democracy due to the neighborhood effect. It is also the place of the civil society where the citizens are expected to socialize. It is a place of letting the political culture live. In this respect, Kıraathane is a means of preserving the national values and local traditions. On the other hand, *Kahvehane* and *Kıraathane*, which are seen as leisure spots, are regarded as a demonstration of unemployment. Just as these spaces are a reflection of the economy, they are also projections of democracy in the public sphere.

In the present work, after giving a historical background about the coffee-houses and public reading houses in Turkey, we will deal with the literature on these spaces from critical theory perspective of Jurgen Habermas. However, these public spaces are often gendered places in which men are predominant. They are places where men seek to give political decisions by talking to their friends. The neighborhood effect can therefore account for the voting behavior of women who are given less opportunity to participate in these spaces because of their gender. Thus, we will examine the public sphere, the voting behavior and the neighborhood effect by taking *Kahvehane* and *Kıraathane* as a case. We will consult the secondary sources in order to examine the case.

In Turkey, the political power (ab)uses coffee-houses and public reading spaces as venues for their political campaigns. In fact, during the campaigns for the general elections on the 24th of June 2018, one of the commitments of the political power was on transforming the *Kıraathane* from places where only rumors are made into those where people read, learn and effect others while enjoying snacks for free.

Keywords: Public Reading Houses (*Kıraathane),* coffee-house (*Kahvehane*), political power, neighborhood effect, voting behavior

INTRODUCTION

In Turkey, during the election campaigns held on the 24th June 2018, reconstruction or redesign of Kıraathane (public reading house) by the ruling party created a lot of debate and even criticized by the opposition parties since Erdogan, the current president of Turkey, stated that it would be designed by the current political power for the youth and snacks would be served free of charge. From the late Ottoman empire and even the beginning of the reign of Suleiman the Magnificent until today, *Kıraathane* and *Kahvehane* have always been public spheres where citizens would talk about politics, sports or just enjoy their free time by having coffee or tea. Today, these mostly masculinized spheres are used for political reasons by the ruling AKP in order to disseminate its ideology and political campaigns benefitting from the neighborhood effect. This is indeed not a novel approach. For instance, Heise (2001, 164) talks about political coffee houses of the 18th century in the US, France and England and points out that coffee houses used to be the public spheres where for example in France, the French revolution was sparked by the talks and speech and political discussion of Voltaire, Rousseau, Diderot, Fontonelle in the coffee houses. The coffee-houses have turned into public spaces as does Habermas indicate, which have today been politicized. In fact, public spaces of Habermas are defined as the spheres where individuals are faced with the state and other political institutions (Özkoçak 2009, 17). Coffee houses were places during the Ottoman Empire where people would talk about the victories and politics of the Sublime Porte. Today, they are also places where politics is profoundly the topic of interest. In fact, these public places are necessary for local democracy in which the citizens decide for which political party to vote, discuss with their friends about the ruling power, economy and even foreign policy. The current political power, aware of the role of the coffeehouses and public reading houses

(*Kıraathane*) in disseminating its political party manifesto or ideology, convincing those who think differently from its own partisans, has today a policy to convert these public places into those of AKP partisans. Public reading houses will be partisan registration places by means of political campaigns or courses taught at these places. At least, the ruling party will interfere in the public sphere of the people, breaking into the private life of the citizens. They will be convinced to/have to vote for the ruling party as a result of the psychological pressure or due to the fear of the discussions. Democratic environment will be ruined, people will be intimidated socially.

Kahvehane and *Kıraathane* have always been spaces for people to have public opinion (Kapani 2017, 164). Opinion leaders with the information they obtain through rumors, newspapers, social media strongly affect the opinion of the citizens in these coffee and public reading houses. Face-to-face talks and discussions are also very effective on political decisions. The present study discusses the *Kıraathane* politics of the ruling party as a public sphere where the AKP could intervene in democracy by means of controlling *Kahvehane* and *Kıraathane* for these main reasons: (1) To manipulate public opinion positively about the political power specifically the youth in these places; (2) to protect its hegemony on the AKP partisans and (3) Recruit new partisans trained in these places by means of courses such as language, religion, history and politics etc. as AKP does not have any systematically trained personnel.

LITERATURE REVIEW

Public Sphere

Public sphere as first stated by Jurgen Habermas in his popular work *Structural Transformation of the Public Sphere* is a bourgeois space (Habermas 2010, 57) for designing a space in modern societies where political participation concretizes by means of discussions (Fraser and Valenta 2001, 129). It is in fact an obligation for deliberative democracy.

Within the framework of deliberative democracy, Rawls advocates that principles of justice, which will be determined by political consensus, and society can reconcile while Habermas contends that political legitimacy can be created by political consensus established by debates in public space, which is equal to each citizen in all respects. Therefore, public space occupies an important place in communicative action (Habermas 1984), a crucial factor in deliberative democracy. While the liberal political order takes place in the feudal order, there is a public space that allows discussion and consensus among the people in order to solve the problems. In this public space, all citizens can freely and critically discuss. Critical discussions of the political power would take place in the coffee houses of England or in the salons of pre-revolutionary France. Satirical literature was born in these salons. New ideas and opinions of revolution like the French revolution resulted in the novel periods of philosophy. The bourgeois public sphere was created by means of egalitarian values and discussions. "Literary criticism adopted a new 'conversational' role as it sought to feed off and back into the discussions taking place in the coffee houses and literary societies" (Goode 2005, 9).

According to Habermas, Lennox, and Lennox (1974, 49), "the public sphere is a realm of social life where public opinion is formed". Therefore, access to this sphere is provided to all citizens. Individuals come together to constitute a public body, which can freely express their own ideology and discuss politics. It is a space where all the citizens debate their own private affairs, and which is therefore institutionalized arena by interactive discussions. Conceptually, this arena is different from the state and thus it is an arena of production and circulation of discourses critical of the state (Fraser and Valenta 2001, 56). It is the only arena where citizens feel free to discuss and decide for political participation and frame their own voting behavior. Fraser (1990, 57) states that "public sphere is the space in which citizens deliberate about their common affairs, hence, an institutionalized arena of discursive interaction. This arena is conceptually distinct from the state; it is a site for the production and circulation of discourses that can in principle be critical of the state". Therefore, free public sphere which does not feel any imposition of the state is closely related with the quality of democracy. It is no doubt possible that individuals we identify as citizens can act as a public sphere only if they can interact with each other without any limitation in their social environment-in other words, with the right to freely express and disseminate their own ideas and establish autonomous group organizations. Such a public sphere becomes the place for public opinion. According to Duman (2010, 357), public sphere does also indicate the civil society that balances the state. Indeed, civil society is defined within the framework of a trium: political society-economic society-civil society and public sphere is an indirect space between the state and the civil society. Public sphere creates a space for questioning the contrast between the civil society and the state from the perspective of modern political theory (Sarıbay 2000, 17). Ardahan (2016, 51) indicates ecological, economic, political, psychological, esthetic, social, educative, symbolic and communicative benefits and roles of the public sphere. For instance, political role of the public sphere serves the citizens to come together for political reasons such as influencing the public opinion or changing the voting behavior as well as political participation. For political scientists, the public space is indeed "a metaphor that refers to the myriad ways in which citizens separated in time and space can participate in collective deliberation, decision-making and action, a concept interchangeable with the public realm" (Parkinson 2009, 101). Today, the meaning of public sphere has transformed from physical space into media and internet. What is important is to deliberate speeches, make decisions and action on the government and the state. Democracy means voting, demonstration, petition, boycotting, arguing and discussing and persuasion briefly political participation, which Young (2002, 213) says takes place in a physical setting to "which anyone has access, a space of openness and exposure".

Neighborhood Effect

In light of the arguments above, neighborhood deeply affects the electoral behavior of voters. It is commonly known that the neighborhood effect should not be ignored in electoral manipulation. Voters are profoundly influenced by the neighborhood in elections or in national issues. For instance, in one study conducted by (Bisgaard, Dinesen, and Sonderskov 2016, 720), it was found that national economic conditions are shaped, measured and controlled "at more aggregate levels (within a radius of 2,500 meters), by municipality characteristics, political ideology, and a host of other individual as well as contextual characteristics, including unemployment within an individual's household."

Family members, friends and workmates are psychologically and socially influenced by conversations on voting decisions. In one important study conducted by Kevin R. Cox (1969), the neighborhood effect was introduced in order to explain the influence of the people on voting decisions. Pattie and Johnston (2000, 42) state that political cues or electoral information are disseminated through social ties and networks and conversations between friends and family members, or, in Cox's term, "acquaintance circles" (Cox 1969, 92). It is suggested that "if the information reaching an individual through her/his conversations predominantly favors one party, then she/he is more likely to vote for that party". The electoral area and its social network create a situation that forms people's decisions on politics (Burbank 1995, 632). Political campaigns in elections certainly have an influence on the voters' decisions; however, social networks can become supportive of the campaigns and even more effective. Partisans directly or indirectly work for a certain political party to win the elections by putting social or psychological pressure on others. Such pressure is contextualized by "personal observation, informal interaction, organizationally based interaction and mass media" (Books and Prysby 1991).

Citizens see their friends and families as political discussants and their "preferences have important consequences for the vote choices of other citizens since vote preferences are socially structured, not only by the characteristics of the voter, but also by the characteristics and preferences of others with whom the voter discusses politics" (Huckfeldt and Sprague 1995, 189), specifically by informal interactions. Miller (1977, 65) explains the "effect of the social environment by contact models: those who speak together vote together." Patterns of the neighborhood effect are also suggested by Johnston et al. (2004, 369), such as "social interaction," whereby people who live together talk together, and "neighborhood selection," whereby people who vote together live together resulting in a halo effect, "neighborhood emulation," whereby people who live together act like each other and "environmental observation," where people are influenced by what they see in their neighborhood, which leads them to vote for a particular party that will promote their own interests, and finally "party mobilization," where people who live together respond together to party campaigns. Consequently, spatial organization is greater than social networks. As stated by Tobler (1970, 236), "everything is related to everything else, but near things are more related than distant things". Party mobilization is in fact possible as long as the masses allow it. Space matters specifically when the campaigns of the parties influence the masses. "Many models of voting behavior and partisan competition have assumed that parties and voters can be located in some simple ideological space" (Feldman 2003, 477). This ideological space is either a cafeteria, coffee-house or a meeting hall.

KIRAATHANE AS A SPACE FOR POLITICAL COMMUNICATION

Kıraathane or public reading houses are places where the public socialize and politicize. These places have lost their true meaning today, which used to be places for reading, *Kıraat* in Arabic and *hane* means house. The public in the Ottoman empire would frequently use *Kıraathane* to read books and discuss politics and daily life in public. As a public sphere, *Kıraathane* has mostly been a place for the civil society, who would express their opinion on the government. For example, during the Ottoman empire, *Kıraathane* was a place to discuss the novelties, conquests, social and political life in public. The ordinary people would also talk about the politics of the government. Some would voluntarily give a speech about the emperor and eulogize the sultanate. Others would just keep silent and blacklist those critical of the government. In the Ottoman empire, the agents of the emperor would get information about a possible riot or revolt against the government in the *Kıraathane*. In the republic of Turkey, the meaning of *Kıraathane* changed due to the official regime, Kemalism and it became a place for passing free time. When the unemployment rate is higher, *Kıraathane* becomes a shelter for the unemployed. In one research, in *Turkey* 1413 public libraries are reported while there are more than 400 thousand coffee/public reading houses[1]. No more reading takes place in these places belonging to the civil society. Today, *Kıraathanes* are also regarded as harmful to children and family life so they can legally be open and must be 100 meters away from schools and public life according to regulation and law[2]. *Kıraathanes* used to be and still are cultural spaces dominated mostly by men in Turkey. The women frequently choose cafeteria instead of manly *Kıraathanes* as they feel uncomfortable. "Coffeehouses sprang up and functioned as important political, social and economic institutions. According to the most popular story, we owe the practice of coffee drinking much to the religious practices of Sufi dervishes" (Bursa 2016). *Kıraathanes* have become an issue of political campaigns in the presidential elections on 24th June 2018 when the president of Turkey and the leader of AKP, Erdogan promised to open "*Kıraathane* of the nation" (*Millet Kıraathanesi*) where people would spend their time doing nothing but participating in the courses taught by AKP partisans and new fans of AKP are accustomed to the party. We are of the opinion that (re)opening the *Kıraathanes* by the ruling party is based on political reasons specifically when AKP has experienced a decrease in its votes and in the number of the party supporters in the last presidential elections due to the domestic and international politics followed by the AKP. For example, the party abandoned the Kurdish opening process as a

---

[1] The number of public libraries and public reading houses http://arsiv.ntv.com.tr/news/95529.asp (Accessed on 04.09.2018). Public reading houses serve today in fact as places to have tea and coffee and not as really reading spaces.
[2] Umuma Açık Yerler ve İçkili Yerler İle Resmî veya Özel Öğretim Kurumları Arasındaki Uzaklıkların Belirlenmesine Dair Yönetmelik http://www.mevzuat.gov.tr/Metin.Aspx?MevzuatKod=7.5.4797&MevzuatIliski=0&sourceXmlSearch= (Accessed on 15.10.2018)

result of the disagreement between HDP, Kurdish People's Democratic Party and AKP. Therefore, AKP lost most of its ethnically Kurdish supporters in the southeastern part of Turkey vis-à-vis HDP's leader, Selahattin Demirtaş in the elections in 2015. The massacre of two policemen by PKK terrorist organization in their house infuriated the president Erdogan and AKP adopted a more anti-Kurdish opening enunciation.

Kıraathanes become day by day the public spaces where civil society is controlled by the political society, whereby democracy is questioned. Based on the Gramscian theory, class system is supported not only by the unequal economic and political power but also bourgeois hegemony and values, which are spread or disseminated by the civil society comprised of media, churches, youth movements and labor unions as well as social environment, thereby the ruling class gains spiritual and cultural superiority (Heywood 2012, 267). The reason why the *Kıraathanes* are targeted by the ruling power is first to maintain its hegemony among the civil society. Secondly, the AKP is interested in consolidating the loyalty of the partisans to the party, by means of their attendance to *Millet Kıraathanes*. These partisans are in search of finding jobs in the public or private sector. *Millet* is the general term for all the supporters of the AKP and Erdogan frequently uses the concept "*Benim milletim*" (my nation) meaning those who support Erdogan and the party and its politics. Koyuncu (2014) for instance states that the concept "*Millet*" for AKP is the people who are conservative-democrat, are following and supporting national values and not critical of the government. *Millet Kıraathane* is therefore specifically for those empathetic to the party and Erdogan. In fact, since these *Kıraathanes* are created and redesigned by the AKP, those who are against its politics would not naturally join the activities conducted by the AKP sympathizers. This leads us to have the opinion that people are classified again. AKP is contributing to the creation of its own bourgeois and supporters by means of *Millet Kıraathane*.

AKP is a party where the progressivists came together in the early 2000s to found the party and recruit members. Since it is a conservative-democratic party, most old democratic conservative members of the parties such DYP (Right Path Party), ANAP (Motherland Party) and conservative nationalists, AKP has still not been able to create its own party alignments. Therefore, AKP always needed the support of the people and was and is still interested in having its own members indoctrinated by the party rules and the leader. The party has sought to get the support of the Turkish *nation* especially after Gezi Park protests, which took place in 2013. In need of new members to make them understand that the party is on the *right path*, AKP creates new areas for partisans and does not refrain from intervening in the civil society.

Governments are often the most influential agent on political socialization though indirectly (Sokullu 2016, 117). Through the control and imposition of its ideology on the coffee and public reading houses, the Turkish government aims to have direct impact on the citizens' political socialization, which is closely linked with conservative-secular life and therefore, voting behavior is deeply influenced by the neoliberal populist policies of the government. Leaders are interested in learning about the political psychology of the citizens since faith, values, ideologies and attitudes are profoundly effective on the voters (Cottam et al. 2010). In one study on Islamic visibilities and public sphere conducted by Göle (2006, 33), coffee-houses are regarded as public spheres where "Muslim stigmatization is reversed to a subaltern superiority and which offer an opportunity to mediate and negotiate Muslims' ambivalences between sameness and difference in respect to modern and secular life-spaces". *Millet Kıraathanes* are the public spaces which are targeted by the Turkish government first to "grow up a religious generation" in Erdogan's terms, where the youth reads and becomes affiliated to the past, Ottoman Empire and Turkish history. In that sense, AKP's understanding of nationalism is closely related with neoliberal nationalism shaped by the discourses such as "serving the nation", "dedication to the nation" instead of pure Kemalist nationalist concepts, which are not comprised of Islamic values and background. Erdogan's "nation" sets forth an Islamic-Turkish nationalism rather than Turkish-Islam synthesis frequently stated and adopted by the nationalist MHP (Nationalist Movement Party). *Millet Kıraathanes* are therefore tools for disseminating the "palatable nationalism" (Öztan 2014), which every ethnicity would agree on.

Millet Kıraathane has been a tool for political campaign during 24 June 2018 elections in Turkey. AKP leader, Erdogan, explained that *Kıraathanes* would be the places to get trained and become more educated while enjoying free tea and snacks. On the contrary, the opposition party presidential candidate, Muharrem Ince, stated that they would be the places for the unemployed to spend their time and become pacified. *Kıraathanes* are therefore the symbols of unemployment as most people in the places spend their time just sitting and waiting for work instead of producing. In Turkey, where the unemployment rate is rising day by day, the political power is intending to control the unemployed from a possible public unrest and prevent another Gezi protest, which started in 2013 as a peaceful protest but turned into an action of overthrowing the government. The neoliberal populist policies of the government are based on construction and not on production. The construction sector is top source of revenue of the government. Since the economy is based on "cement" and not on industry, there is a high rate of unemployment. The indicator of unemployment is the number of *Kıraathane.* According to Turkish Statistical Institute (TUIK), people read less than spending time in the *Kıraathane.* The government is encouraging assisting the courses in the *Millet Kıraathane* instead of favoring, facilitating and encouraging the use of public libraries. Public libraries are in fact not efficiently used like those in the USA, which is a part of the American culture. Unlike those in the USA, public libraries are frequently used by the high school students preparing for the university entrance exam. *Millet Kıraathanes* replace these libraries for these students in order to increase the popularity of the AKP among the young electorate. Those who already have a link with the AKP exert an influence on others that commence knowing AKP. The neighborhood effect helps the latter get affiliated to the party through the *Kıraathane* effect in such a way that "*Benim milletim*" emerges.

CONCLUSION

Kıraathane was a political issue and argument in the last presidential elections on 24 June 2018 between the political power and the opposition party. The political power indicated the redesign and reopening of the *Millet Kıraathane*, which would serve people for free so that they read and get free courses of history, religion and politics. *Millet Kıraathanes* are becoming day by day places for the ruling party to find new partisans, maintain its hegemony on the existing members, controlling those potentially unemployed and threat to the government in the *Kıraathane* and finally creating its own bourgeois and electorate. We can see that "Erdogan is in favor of creating his own "nation". It is important that this nation is independent of western powers, owns its own will, is able to produce its own products locally and nationally. However, this is created through the hegemony of the political power. *Kıraathane* is therefore one of the spaces for this hegemony. In the *Kıraathane*, those intending to have a job would find an opportunity to meet those of the party in bureaucracy, who would be reference for them to have a job in the government. *Millet Kıraathanes* become therefore reference points for getting to know the potential candidates for governance, bureaucracy or just business. The civil society in Turkey spends their time in these *Kıraathanes* and becomes partisans, who use the neighborhood effect to exert influence on the voters.

REFERENCES

Ardahan, Faik. 2016. "Kamusal Bir Mekân Olan Memleket Kahvelerinin Tercih Edilme Nedenleri ve Rekreasyonel Önemi (Recreational Importance and Reasons for being Preferred of Countryman Coffee Stall as Communal Place)." *Igdir University Journal of Social Sciences* 1 (9):49-69.

Bisgaard, M., P. T. Dinesen, and K. M. Sonderskov. 2016. "Reconsidering the Neighborhood Effect: Does Exposure to Residential

Unemployment Influence Voters' Perceptions of the National Economy?" *Journal of Politics* 78 (3):719-732. doi: 10.1086/685088.

Books, John W., and Charles L. Prysby. 1991. *Political behavior and the local context*. New York: Praeger.

Burbank, M. J. 1995. "The Psychological Basis of Contextual Effects." *Political Geography* 14 (6-7):621-655. doi: Doi 10.1016/0962-6298(95)00057-H.

Bursa, Nihal. 2016. *Brewing Pots of Revolt: Coffeehouses*. Dublin Gastronomy Symposium.

Cottam, Martha L, Elena Mastors, Thomas Preston, and Beth Dietz. 2010. *Introduction to political psychology*: Psychology Press.

Cox, Kevin R. 1969. "The voting decision in a spatial context" *Progress in Geography* 1:81-117.

Duman, Fatih. 2010. "Sivil toplum" ["Civil Society"] In *Siyaset*, edited by Mümtaz'er Türköne, 347-377. İstanbul: Opus.

Feldman, Stanley. 2003. "Values, ideology, and the structure of political attitudes." In *The Oxford handbook of political psychology*, edited by Leonie Huddy, David O. Sears and Robert Jervis, 477-508. Oxford: Oxford University Press.

Fraser, Nancy. 1990. "Rethinking the public sphere: A contribution to the critique of actually existing democracy." *Social text* (25/26):56-80.

Fraser, Nancy, and Muriel Valenta. 2001. "Repenser la sphère publique: une contribution à la critique de la démocratie telle qu'elle existe réellement. [Rethinking the public sphere: a contribution to the critique of democracy as it really exists.] " *Hermès, La Revue* (3):125-156.

Goode, Luke. 2005. *Jürgen Habermas: democracy and the public sphere*, *Modern European thinkers*. London; Ann Arbor, MI: Pluto Press.

Göle, Nilüfer. 2006. "Islamic visibilities and Public Sphere." In *Islam in public: Turkey, Iran and Europe*, edited by Nilüfer Göle and Ludwig Ammann, 3-45. İstanbul: İstanbul Bilgi University Press.

Habermas, Jürgen. 1984. *The theory of communicative action*. Vol. 2: Beacon press.

Habermas, Jürgen. 2010. *Kamusallığın yapısal dönüşümü [Structural Transformation of the Public Sphere]*. Translated by Tanıl Bora and Mithat Sancar. İstanbul: İletişim Yayınları.

Habermas, Jürgen, Sara Lennox, and Frank Lennox. 1974. "The public sphere: An encyclopedia article (1964)." *New German Critique* (3):49-55.

Heise, Ulla. 2001. *Kahve ve Kahvehane [Coffee and Public Reading House]*. Ankara: Dost Kitabevi.

Heywood, Andrew. 2012. *Siyaset [Politics]*. Translated by Bekir Berat Özipek, Bican Şahin, Mete Yıldız-Bican Şahin, Zeynep Kopuzlu, Bahattin Seçilmişoğlu and Atilla Yayla. Ankara: Adres Publications.

Huckfeldt, R. Robert, and John D. Sprague. 1995. *Citizens, politics, and social communication: information and influence in an election campaign, Cambridge studies in political psychology and public opinion*. Cambridge England; New York: Cambridge University Press.

Johnston, R., K. Jones, R. Sarker, S. Burgess, and A. Bolster. 2004. "Party support and the neighbourhood effect: spatial polarisation of the British electorate, 1991-2001." *Political Geography* 23 (4):367-402. doi: 10.1016/j.polgeo.2003.12.008.

Kapani, Münci. 2017. *Politika bilimine giriş [Introduction to political science]*. Ankara: BB101 Yayınları.

Koyuncu, Büke. 2014. *"Benim milletim...": AK Parti iktidarı, din ve ulusal kimlik [My nation...: AKP Power, Religion and National Identity]*. 1. Baskı. ed, *Araştırma-inceleme dizisi*. İstanbul: İletişim Yayınları.

Miller, William Lockley. 1977. *Electoral dynamics in Britain since 1918*. London: Macmillan.

Özkoçak, Selma Akyazıcı. 2009. "Kamusal Alanın Üretim Sürecinde Erken Modern İstanbul Kahvehaneleri" ["Early modern Istanbul Coffee-houses in the production of Public Sphere"] In *Osmanlı kahvehaneleri: mekân, sosyalleşme, iktidar*, edited by Yaşar Ahmet, 17-35. İstanbul: Kitap Yayınevi.

Öztan, Güven Gürkan. 2014. "The struggle for hegemony between Turkish nationalisms in the neoliberal era." In *Turkey Reframed: Constituting*

Neoliberal Hegemony, edited by İsmet Akaç, Ahmet Bekmen and Barış Alp Özden, 75-92. London: Pluto Press.

Parkinson, John R. 2009. "Does democracy require physical public space?" In *Does Truth Matter? Democracy and Public Space*, edited by Raf Geenens and Ronald Tinnevelt, 101-114. Springer.

Pattie, Charles, and Ron Johnston. 2000. ""People who talk together vote together": An exploration of contextual effects in Great Britain." *Annals of the Association of American Geographers* 90 (1):41-66. doi: Doi 10.1111/0004-5608.00183.

Sarıbay, Ali Yaşar. 2000. *Kamusal alan, diyalojik demokrasi, sivil itiraz [Public Sphere, Dialogical Democracy and Civil Opposition]*: Alfa Yayınları.

Sokullu, Ebru Ş Canan. 2016. "Siyasal Kültür" ["Political Culture"]. In *Karşılaştırmalı Siyaset Temel Konular ve Yaklaşımlar*, edited by Sabri Sayarı and Hasret Dikici Bilgin, 101-121. İstanbul: İstanbul Bilgi Üniversitesi Yayınları.

Tobler, Waldo R. 1970. "A computer movie simulating urban growth in the Detroit region." *Economic geography* 46 (sup1):234-240.

Young, Iris Marion. 2002. *Inclusion and democracy*: Oxford University Press on Demand.

In: A Closer Look at Political Communication   ISBN: 978-1-53615-321-7
Editor: Mark H. Tatum   © 2019 Nova Science Publishers, Inc.

Chapter 3

RACIALIZED METAPHORS AS POLITICAL COMMUNICATION: PUTTING THE U.S. "CARAVAN CRISIS" IN HISTORICAL PERSPECTIVE

Johnny Holloway*, *PhD*
School of Public Affairs, American University, Washington, DC, US

ABSTRACT

The fiery language of Donald Trump – as both candidate and sitting president – regarding immigration and immigrants from Latin America (e.g., as rapists, murderers, invaders) has made headlines and sparked controversy. Characterizing illegal immigrants (and Latin people more broadly) in speeches, at rallies, and in the media in terms of violence, criminality, and as threats to national security, President Trump has been accused of employing a race-based crisis strategy to appeal to the fears and insecurities of white voters. However, to depict this type of political communication as somehow anomalous or otherwise unique to this administration and its specific goals misses the mark. Any effort to

* Corresponding Author Email: holloway@american.edu.

understand the key logics at play that make such a modern strategy both possible and potentially effective must place its analysis firmly within a larger historical context. Demonstrably, the usage of racialized metaphors - like invasion and infection – has been a cornerstone of United States policy towards those south of the border. Conceptions of Latin peoples as inferior and as a source of menace have been foundational elements of U.S. – Latin America relations throughout its nearly 200-year history. Clearly articulated in the Monroe Doctrine, these taken for granted themes figured prominently in a consistent foreign policy of direct and indirect interventions in the 19th and 20th centuries designed to ensure United States dominance within the hemisphere. Informed by a discourse theoretical methodology, this chapter focuses on the past use of racialized language as one mechanism for evaluating political communication in the 21st century. Specifically, it illuminates this contemporary "caravan crisis" of Central American refugees by locating it within the broader historical pattern of metaphors employed in the construction of U.S. foreign policy toward Latin America.

Keywords: political communication, Donald Trump, immigration, discourse analysis, metaphor, race, U.S. foreign policy, refugees

INTRODUCTION

This chapter centers on the representations of the recent migrant caravans of Central Americans passing through Mexico on their way to the United States by the Trump administration as an element of its apparent racialized discursive strategy encompassing refugees and immigration policy overall. The nature of President Trump's response to the migrant "crisis" is located within the larger pattern of his statements and actions regarding Latin America, its peoples, and race. Its relative strength is considered. Working from a discourse theoretical perspective, the greater socio-political and historical context (shaping the Trump administrations' interpretations of, and responses to, this crisis) is presented in the form of a "history of the present." It is argued that the effectiveness and therefore the possibility of this discourse cannot be understood outside the specific "common sense" instantiated in the United States via a consistent pattern of historical representations of Latin America[1] and its peoples as inherently inferior and a source of threat.

The so-called caravans informally organized to help shepherd refugees from Central America into and across Mexico had been taking place for years as a form of social action and humanitarian support. These annual, small-scale movements of a few dozen to a few hundred people were not considered a crisis before a news report in the spring of 2018 caught President Trump's attention and fueled his public ire (deCordoba and Whelan 2018; Linthicum 2018). Over the following months, the caravans were said by the White House (without evidence) to contain terrorists and gang members seeking to infiltrate the country (Blake 2018; Schneider, Sands, and Shortell 2018). The Trump administration's representations of this movement of disparate men, women, and children from Latin America as a "crisis," an "onslaught," and an "invasion," would ultimately lead to the ongoing deployment of thousands of United States active duty armed forces personnel near the southern border in support of an actual military mission – Operation Faithful Patriot (Caldwell 2018b; Montoya-Galvez 2019; Youssef 2018a).

However, as it has been well documented, this type of discursive strategy is nothing new for Donald Trump. His prolific use of racialized narratives highlighting a (good) American "self" and a (bad) foreign "other" at the national level did not start during his tenure as president nor even during the 2016 presidential campaign process. Instead, it began in 2011, as Trump enthusiastically embraced (despite the lack of any evidence) the conspiracy theory that Barack Obama had not been born in Hawaii and was therefore not legitimately the president of the United States. This appeal to "birtherism" during televised interviews and other media events served to raise Trump's national profile and initial poll numbers amongst the field of potential 2012 Republican presidential candidates until he decided to drop out of the running (Collinson and Diamond 2016; Parker and Edar 2016). When he chose to enter the 2016

---

[1] In this chapter, Latin and Latin American are used to refer to people residing (past or present) in Mexico, Central America, South America, and the Caribbean. Latino is used to refer to people of Latin American descent residing in the United States.

presidential race on the Republican ticket, Mexico and Latin America figured prominently in Trump's official announcement speech – as enemies of the United States sending in drugs, crime, and rapists (Time Staff 2015). In a June 2016 CNN television interview, candidate Trump repeatedly argued that the American born judge overseeing the case against Trump University was "a Mexican" and thus could not be trusted to rule impartially (Wolf 2017). First candidate and later President Trump consistently seized on individual cases of crimes committed by illegal immigrants as evidence of a widescale movement of criminals, drug dealers, and rapists across the Mexican border necessitating the construction of a fortified wall (Lee 2015; Rizzo 2018). Decrying the number of immigrants coming from "shithole countries" like Haiti and El Salvador, President Trump has advocated for more immigration from nations like Norway (Dawsey 2018).

The fiery language of Donald Trump – as both candidate and sitting president – regarding immigration and immigrants from Latin America (e.g., as rapists, murderers, invaders) has regularly made headlines and sparked controversy. Depicting illegal immigrants (and Latin people more broadly) in speeches, at rallies, and in the media in terms of violence, criminality, and as threats to national security, President Trump has been accused of employing a race-based crisis strategy to appeal to the fears and insecurities of white voters (Obeidallah 2018; Shear and Hirschfeld Davis 2018). Clearly, there has been and continues to be a demonstrable pattern of racialized discourses emanating from the White House seeking to define and divide "good" Americans and "bad" foreigners/others. The migrant caravans are simply the latest target. However, to depict this form of political communication as somehow anomalous or otherwise unique to this President, this administration, or even this (Republican) political party misses the mark. Likewise, simply investigating the reasons why the Trump administration chooses these types of discursive practices (and not others) to inform, organize, and persuade the American public on the subject of immigrant caravans approaching the southern border effectively restricts the scope of inquiry. Instead, any effort to understand the key logics at play in this particular discursive strategy must place its analysis firmly within a larger historical context.

METHODS

To explore this issue, this chapter uses a discourse theoretical approach rooted in a social constructionist philosophy. As such, it takes as its starting point that human access to reality is always through language (Jørgensen and Phillips 2002; Phillips and Hardy 2002). Knowledge is understood as "historically and culturally specific and contingent" (Jørgensen and Phillips 2002, 5) and therefore information derived through discourse research is assumed to be partial, situated (in the specific contexts outlined), and relative (to the researcher's views and values) (Taylor 2001). "Discourse is shaped by situational, institutional and social contexts and at the same time it influences socio-political reality. Social roles, identities, interpersonal reactions and social conditions are constituted through discourse" (Krotofil and Motak 2018). Discourses, consequently, can be understood as sets of socially and historically constructed rules that fix meanings by effectively designating what is and what is not (Carabine 2001). In this way, power (in this discursive context) is both enabling in that it creates the social order in which humans live and constraining in that it creates that same particular social order by excluding all alternative possibilities (Jørgensen and Phillips 2002). For example, the characterization of the members of the migrant caravans by the Trump administration as "gang members" or "terrorists" works to logically establish them as enemies or invaders (as opposed to "refugees" or "Christians" who would conversely logically deserve aid and compassion). In sum, according to Milliken (1999), "discourses are understood to work to define and to enable, and also to silence and to exclude, for example, by limiting and restricting authorities and experts to some groups, but not others, endorsing a certain common sense, but making other modes of categorizing and judging meaningless, impracticable, inadequate or otherwise disqualified" (229).

Discourses are comprised of *texts* – a loose term that encompasses a broad range of semiotic forms including written documents, spoken words, interviews, pictures, symbols, survey data, and observed and unobserved social practices (Hansen and Sørensen 2005; Howarth and Torfing 2005; Stillar 1998). Here, relevant examples of texts would include things like Donald Trump's tweets and rally speeches, executive orders and official documents produced by the administration, and media interviews with cabinet members and presidential staff. Discourses are located and performed in a variety of texts, yet they exist beyond the individual texts that constitute them. Texts are made meaningful only via their interrelation with other texts, the different discourses on which they draw, and the manner of their construction, distribution, and consumption (Phillips and Hardy 2002). Moreover, discourses, like texts, possess no independent meaning. Instead, they are made meaningful by virtue of their location in and relation to their broader historical and social context (Reisigl and Wodak 2001). Therefore, the study of discourse can be envisioned as three dimensional as texts are connected to discourses, that are placed in historical and social context, and serve as reference points for the specific actors, relationships, and procedures that distinguish the particular issue under examination (Phillips and Hardy 2002).

Since knowledge is historically and culturally specific and contingent, different discourses work continuously to fix and define specific meanings and identities while denying others. An *order of discourse* represents a social space where two or more discourses partly encompass the same terrain, the meanings of which they struggle to hegemonize (Fairclough 1998; Jørgensen and Phillips 2002). Hegemonic or dominant discourses fix meanings by naturalizing, by creating a "common sense" that circumscribes all action in that sphere (Epstein 2008; Torfing 2005). In this sense, the migrant caravans can be seen as one element of the larger immigration order of discourse where the specific practices and activities of President Trump and his administration constitute one discourse struggling (against others) for dominance. In an immediate, anecdotal fashion, the relative power of Donald Trump's discursive strategy (e.g., continuously trumpeting the threat of "open borders" and the need for a wall, representing refugees as gang members) can be readily assessed. In addition to winning the presidency, Trump continues to command the loyalty of the overwhelming majority of Republican voters and Republican elected officials. He maintains significant support from Latino voters. His fortified border and militarized immigration strategy has even engendered the support of some prominent Democratic senators. Finally, Trump has deployed thousands of active duty military personnel to the border with Mexico – after 17 years of the War on Terror and during the Christmas holiday season – with minimal protest from the general public and legislators (Blake 2018; Cortes 2018; Krogstad, Flores, and Lopez 2018; Leary 2018; Oliphant 2018; Richards 2018; Zhou 2018; Zurcher 2018). A more comprehensive study could fully analyze this order of discourse in order to determine its scope and the nature of its competing discourses, but such a study is beyond the capacity of this work. As noted, however, the different discourses within a specified order of discourse can never be divorced from the historical and cultural context in which those discourses are located. To this end, I seek to contextualize the discursive practices of the Trump administration – to reveal the logics that create its intelligibility – with a genealogical account of United States relations with Latin America operating as a specific "history of the present."

A HISTORY OF THE PRESENT

According to Campbell (1998), "a history of the present exhibits an unequivocally contemporary orientation. Beginning with an incitement from the present – an acute manifestation of a ritual of power – this mode of analysis seeks to trace how such rituals of power arose, took shape, gained importance, and effected politics. In short, this mode of analysis asks how certain terms and concepts have historically functioned within discourse" (5-6). This approach orients the researcher towards the contingent and perspectival nature of history by problematizing the various social processes that constituted its particular "truths" while precluding other possibilities (see also Howarth 2000; Jackson 2006). Predating the

American Revolution and continuing into the present day, the "truth" of a superior American Self and an inferior Latin Other is an integral element of United States policies in the Western Hemisphere (Johnson 1990; Pike 1992). However, these policies cannot be seen simply as the rational and self-interested actions of a preexisting and fully realized nation. Instead, a genealogical approach highlights how the functions of United States policy constitute part of a continuous process of identity formation where negative characterizations of Latin peoples work to identify "America" by circumscribing *them* in order to define *us*. Drawing on a previous study (Holloway 2012), this section begins with the three factors comprising the root of historical American perceptions of Latin America and its citizens – the Black Legend, the Color Line, and the State of Nature.

The Black Legend

The origins of American views on the peoples of Latin America lie in cultural and religious prejudices leveled against Spain by the English beginning in the 16th century. A summary of charges – later called the Black Legend[2] – held that the Spanish were responsible for widespread religious persecution (embodied in the Spanish Inquisition), a genocidal imperial campaign in their conquest of the Americas, and the brutal exploitation of its indigenous populations (Johnson 1990). These views found great purchase among American settlers and were reinforced throughout this era by the widely available works of authors like Richard Hakluyt and Thomas Gage (Hunt 1987; Johnson 1990). Even after independence from England, these beliefs did not waver. When the Iberian colonies in the Americas began to rebel in 1808, the Black Legend viewpoint was also implicated in the vacillating United States response. While Spain was decidedly wicked from the view of the United States, it was the Iberian heritage of the revolutionaries that made their republican bona fides and their ability to govern any future states suspect in the minds

---

[2] For more details on the Black Legend, see Keen (1969).

of the American elite like Thomas Jefferson and John Quincy Adams (Langley 2010; Schoultz 1998; Smith 2005). From their birth, the countries of Latin America were tarred by their blood and cultural ties to the Iberian Peninsula. Their inhabitants were consequently stereotyped as "superstitious, obstinate, lazy, cowardly, vain, pretentious, dishonest, unclean, impractical, and corrupt" (Hunt 1987, 59). Nevertheless, Spanish blood was not the sole criterion for this calculated opprobrium.

The Color Line

By 1830, the new Latin America republics had been officially recognized as independent of Spain. Also by this time, racial consciousness had firmly developed in the in the United States. Most Americans had come to believe in the primacy of a distinct Anglo-Saxon race – to which they belonged – whose very blood was the driving force behind its continuous military, political, and economic triumphs (Horsman 1998). Sitting atop a perceived racial hierarchy with the darkest (and least fit) at its base and the lightest (and most able) at its apex, the United States of the 19th century was obsessed with the color line and reacted severely when it was not observed – "the darker the complexion of the people in question, the sharper was the attack" (Hunt 1987, 59). Prevailing prejudices against miscegenation ill-prepared Anglo-Americans for the universal profligacy of interracial sex in Latin America (Johnson 1990). American policymakers had already had their racial fears stoked by the successful slave rebellion in Haiti in 1804. Reports of mindless violence and destruction in its aftermath predisposed the United States to view the political strife and economic stagnation of the newly formed Latin countries as the inevitable result of their racial impurity (Pike 1992). From this perspective, their intermixing with African slaves and the indigenous populations of their countries imbued Latins with the savagery and inhumanity already deemed intrinsic to those races (Hunt 1987).

The State of Nature

That their racial composition (i.e., a mixture of Spanish, indigenous, and African blood) essentially marked them as subhuman is at the core of United States' representations of Latin peoples and thus Latin America. Pike (1992) expounds on these representations in his articulation of the "state of nature" concept. Beginning with the earliest Anglo-Saxon colonization of America, the settlers equated the natural with anarchy, savagery, and the loss of control and viewed it as a thing to be feared, dominated, and ultimately eliminated. Consequently, those who lived in harmony with (or otherwise seemed attuned to) it were immediately suspect. From this perspective, Pike argues, the mark of civilization was the ability to contain and control nature, not only the wildness of the external world embodied in untamed forests and unexplored ranges but also the wildness inherent in human nature and rampant personal desires. This was something white men could do but of which the Native American was simply incapable. Identified even more closely with the state of nature, enslaved blacks offered even greater evidence of the superiority of Anglo-Saxons and the importance of maintaining racial purity (Johnson 1990).

It was with these views of the red and black races, and the knowledge of widespread miscegenation in the new republics, that the United States began to seriously engage Latin America.

Destined to Lead

Long before journalist John O'Sullivan coined the phrase "Manifest Destiny" in 1845, American elites had recognized the exceptional nature of the United States and its divinely ordained future as a transcontinental power. Alexander Hamilton envisioned a hemispheric America capable of dictating terms to the Old World (Kenworthy 1995). Both Thomas Jefferson and John Quincy Adams embraced the vision of a northern continental United States made up of one nation with a uniform culture and political philosophy extending to some or all of the territory of Latin

America (Kenworthy 1995; McDougall 1997). The Monroe Doctrine served as a global announcement that the New World would be regulated by a new form of government – republicanism. These were the architects of the hegemonic tradition of American policy towards Latin America that continues to hold sway in modern times (Schoultz 1998).

Viewed in historical context, Manifest Destiny was the exercise of the long standing American teleology embodied in Monroe's document (Johnson 1990). Its power having advanced significantly by the mid-1840s, the United States was then able to speed up the inevitable. Marching under the banner of Manifest Destiny, President James Polk's administration annexed Texas and wrested away half of Mexico's territory after provoking that neighboring *republic* into war and crushing it militarily (Langley 1989). By 1848, the United States controlled the American southwest and had effectively become a continental power. For the expansionists in the United States coveting the southwest territories, it was the essential savagery of the Mexican people (e.g., "colored mongrel race"; "imbecile and indolent race"; "ignorant, prejudiced, and perfectly faithless"; "aboriginal Indians") that voided their territorial claims and decided their fate (Hunt 1987, 60). These discursive representations of Latins as savage (at worst) or simply inferior (at best) worked not only to define Latin America but also to define and position the United States as leader in relation to the rest of the hemisphere. America, as a white Anglo-Saxon nation, was inherently superior to any and all of the Latin republics (Pike 1992; Schoultz 1998).

However, victory in the war with Mexico dealt a crippling blow to the expansionists' dreams of the United States extending into the southern hemisphere. Perceptions of that population as "part Negro, part Indian, filthy and greasy in appearance" quickly coined a catch-all phrase for Mexicans – greasers (Pike 1992, 100). To annex all (and not just the sparsely settled north) of Mexico would mean incorporating into America the same half-breed, misanthropic, and backwards people that had earned such derision in the run up to the war. Observance of the color line soundly overcame the expansionist credo and the movement to annex all of Mexico quickly dissolved (Langley 1989; Schoultz 1998).

This tension – between America's belief in its ordained civilizing mission and its natural hemispheric leadership on the one hand and its belief in Latin inferiority and the dangers of racial pollution on the other – was again present in the circumstances leading to the Spanish American War. "Contemplating events on their southern doorstep in the closing years of the nineteenth century, Americans saw alien disorder; savage Spanish colonial rule in Cuba and Puerto Rico, lawless frontier lands in Central America. There were two ways to respond: go in and clean these countries up, or stay out for fear of being contaminated" (Black 1988, 11). The American forces in this conflict, many of whom were veterans of the Civil War and the military campaigns against the Native Americans in the plains states, brought the historical color line along with flag to the Caribbean and the Philippines. To the occupying forces, the Filipinos were "niggers," "gugus," "black devils," "Apaches," and "Comanches" (Krenn 2006, 48; Weston 1998, 303). Not surprisingly, the Cuban and Filipino contribution to the victory over Spain was never acknowledged by the United States[3] (Schoultz 1998).

The defeat of Spain in 1898 set off a battle between the imperialist and anti-imperialist political blocs in the United States. Again, both sides shared a view of the peoples in question as less than human. The anti-imperialism forces argued that America would suffer the contaminating effects of their primitive cultures should it incorporate former Spanish colonies (Pike 1992). The supporters of imperialism argued that the United States by its greatness would civilize these lesser peoples (Hunt 1987). The pro-imperialism forces proved victorious with Cuba, Puerto Rico, and the Philippines becoming literal or de facto American possessions (Langley 1989). Consistently represented in text and image[4] as "children," it was understood that these former colonies would require both tutelage and a firm hand (Pérez 2008).

---

[3] Consider that even the name of the conflict – the Spanish-American War – rejects the status of the Cubans and Filipinos as legitimate combatants and completely denies their role in the ultimate victory over Spain.

[4] For a detailed review of the consistent historical representations of Latins and Latin American in United States media images (e.g., political cartoons), see Black (1988) and Johnson (1980).

The terms of the victory over Spain made the United States an imperial power and also cemented American views about Latin America. Ultimately, fear of contamination made the outright incorporation of additional territory and their populations into the United States unthinkable and thus impossible (Schoultz 1998). However, this did nothing to stifle American efforts towards regional hegemony in the 20th century which were carried out through a combination of economic and military means (Livingstone 2009).

Roosevelt Corollary to the Good Neighbor Policy

American perceptions of Latin states as infantile – and as such unreliable, defenseless, and in need of direct supervision – were heavily implicated in the long series of direct and indirect United States interventions in Latin America in the 20th century. Cuba's "independence" in 1902 came only with assurances of continued American control built into its constitution. In addition to the right to intervene militarily at will, the United States was given power over Cuba's treaty-making and foreign borrowing decisions as well as rights to military bases. (Ninkovich 2001, 98). In the discursive spaces created by the child metaphor, "disciplining offspring is an act of love, not power" (Kenworthy 1995, 31). As such, United States actions towards Cuba (like the military interventions in 1906 and 1912) were not considered the exercise of American control but rather the dutiful dispensation of parental authority (Pérez 2008). This pattern of control over (and concurrent interventions in) the island remained essentially the same until the late 1950s (Ninkovich 2001; Pérez 2008).

Piqued by Colombia's refusal to accept American terms on a trans-isthmus canal, in 1903 the Roosevelt administration showed up the "jackrabbits," "greedy little anthropoids," and "Dagoes in Bogota" by orchestrating – complete with American naval support – the secession of that country's northernmost province. The new state of Panama received official American diplomatic recognition less than two hours after announcing its independence and with United States recognition came an immediate canal agreement (Ninkovich 2001, 108-110). President Roosevelt justified this intervention in part by arguing that Colombia had proven itself incapable of controlling its territory and therefore America's actions served the interests of civilization (Schoultz 1998).

Latins were perceived as too close to nature, too uncivilized, and consequently could not be trusted to make the right decisions in important matters. The Roosevelt Corollary to the Monroe Doctrine (put forth in 1904) enshrined the principle of direct American intervention in the affairs of Latin American states deemed to have fallen off the path of civilization. The United States would act as regional policeman, in the words of Roosevelt, to "show those Dagos[5] that they will have to behave decently" (quoted in Livingstone 2009, 15). Internal instability and runaway foreign debt that courted European involvement would not be tolerated.

American suzerainty was also exercised through economic mechanisms. When a foreign debt crisis erupted in the Dominican Republic in 1904, the United States had no faith in that country's leadership. Noted one American diplomat, "In times of stress they practically revert to more primitive ways of thinking and acting. In a word they are like children" (quoted in Schoultz 1998, 188). Succumbing to American pressure, the Dominican Republic signed away its customs rights in 1905. When a subsequent administration in 1916 refused to relinquish control over its customs, treasury, and military, American forces seized control and occupied the country for eight years (Livingstone 2009). The implementation of these policies, argues Schoultz (1998), set the stage for President Taft's Dollar Diplomacy and established the common wisdom still governing modern American perceptions of Latin America – only the guidance of the United States prevents the region from devolving into economic chaos.

Between 1903 and 1934, under the aegis of the Roosevelt Corollary to the Monroe Doctrine and Dollar Diplomacy, the United States engaged in military interventions and/or occupations in Cuba (1906-1909; 1912; 1917-

---

[5] According to Schoultz (1998), "'Dago,' a corruption of the Spanish 'Diego,' was originally used in the mid-19th century as a derogatory reference to Mexican men in the U.S. Southwest" (177).

1922), the Dominican Republic (1904; 1914; 1916-1924), Guatemala (1920), Haiti (1915-1934), Honduras (1907; 1911; 1912; 1919; 1924; 1925), Mexico (1913; 1914; 1916-1917; 1918-1919), Nicaragua (1909-1910; 1912-1925; 1926-1933), and Panama (1903-1914; 1921; 1925) (Livingstone 2009). Discursive constructions of these states as home to truculent children or bestial savages were consistently implicated in these policy decisions. For example, the need for the continued occupation of Haiti after securing control of the country's customs in 1915 was justified by American military officials because that country's residents, no matter their outward appearance, were "savage under the skin" and could "revert in a few minutes to the mental state of a savage in the heart of Africa" (Schoultz 1998, 254). Taft's Assistant Secretary of State argued that Dollar Diplomacy's object was "to create a material prosperity which should wean the Central Americans from their usual preoccupation of revolution" (Holden and Zolov 2000, 118).

By the mid-1930s, the economic contraction forced by the Great Depression set limits on available funds to deploy American troops and on the patience of the American public for interventions abroad. Under the auspices of Franklin Roosevelt's Good Neighbor Policy, the United States had signed declarations renouncing its right to intervene in the states of the region, abrogated the Platt Amendment, set limits on its actions in Panama, and ended its long running occupations of Haiti and Nicaragua (Livingstone 2009). "There was however, relatively little change in the underlying belief in the inferiority of Latin American peoples, a condition that was usually attributed to a combination of climatic, racial, and cultural handicaps" (Ninkovich 2001, 143). Moreover, better public relations notwithstanding, American efforts at regional hegemony did not diminish. Instead, less overt mechanisms of control were employed (Schoultz 1998). The United States came to increasingly rely on indigenous authoritarian leaders (e.g., Somoza in Nicaragua) to quell domestic unrest, protect American investments, and to ensure regional stability (Livingstone 2009).

World War II and the Cold War

In the years immediately prior to America's entrance into World War II, the United States, fearing Nazi adventurism, began to establish strong ties with the militaries of all Latin American states by establishing American military advisory groups and opening its military academies to students from throughout the region. After the war, these links would prove a ready means of transplanting America's Cold War ideology to those same militaries (Schoultz 1998). During the war, Latin America, with its supply of vital raw materials (e.g., oil, tin, copper), was of vital strategic importance to the United States (Livingstone 2009). What was not in high demand to support the war effort was the services of the Latin Americans themselves. By the end of the war, the familiar disparaging stereotypes of Latin Americans that had been played down in the Good Neighbor era reemerged once again in the public sphere and popular media (Pike 1992).

The Cold War saw a return to active United States intervention in the region. While fear of communist expansion had replaced concerns about reactionary European power, the guiding principles of American regional hegemony and Latin American subordination remained. Although the Latin American republics sought economic developmental assistance from the United States akin to the Marshall Plan, aid on that scale was reserved for the modern, civilized states of Europe (Langley 1989). Instead, Latin America received in 1947 a regional defense treaty (the Rio Pact) and in a 1948 a regional intergovernmental organization (the Organization of American States) that were both designed to promote an anti-communist agenda in – and foster American control of – the hemisphere (McPherson 2006). The promotion of democracy, conversely, was never genuinely considered for Latin American states because – as children – they were not deemed capable of that system of government. Writing in *Foreign Affairs* in 1950, a member of the State Department's Policy Planning opined that Latin Americans were too wild, too child-like in nature and so lacked the requisite temperament for democracy (Halle 1950).

That same year, George Kennan, the architect of America's strategy to contain Soviet expansion, toured Latin America. In the trip report subsequently filed, he concurred that the peoples of the region could not be trusted with a republican system of government (Holden and Zolov 2000). "It is better to have a strong regime in power than a liberal government if it is indulgent and penetrated by Communists" (quoted in McPherson 2006, 24). Not surprisingly, Washington was content to support any compliant government in the region with the proper anti-communist credentials. Conversely, if any government appeared to deviate in any way from rigid anti-communism, its behavior was deemed a legitimate justification for American intervention.

When President Arbenz of Guatemala initiated a program of moderate agrarian reform, the Eisenhower administration perceived it as a threat to America's regional leadership and prestige. Via a concerted diplomatic, economic, and clandestine military strategy, Arbenz was driven from power in 1954 (Grow 2008). From the seeds of this intervention grew a bloody civil war that would last for 36 years and kill hundreds of thousands of Guatemalans (Livingstone 2009). In Cuba, after the overthrow of the dictator Batista in 1959, Washington's initial cautious optimism was replaced with shock and anger by Fidel Castro's fiery denunciations of America's historical suzerainty over the island and his plans to radically restructure Cuban society (Langley 1989). Long wrapped in the mythos of its selfless sacrifice to liberate Cuba from Spain, policymakers saw Castro's attack on America's civilizing mission as the basest ingratitude and a sure sign of irrationality (Brenner and Castro 2009). This, combined with Castro's leftist policies, spurred calls in the United States to intervene *to protect the Cubans from themselves*. "The logical conclusion of North American claims was that Cubans could not be permitted to squander the freedom that the United States – at such great cost – had obtained for them in 1898" (Pérez 2008, 225). While its failure was widely viewed as embarrassing, few questioned the propriety of the American sponsored invasion of Cuba in 1961 (Black 1988).

The Kennedy administration's response to the success of the Cuban revolution was a dramatic restructuring of military and economic aid to the region. The orientation of military support shifted from hemispheric defense to a focus on internal security and the need "to fight Castro-type guerrilla insurgencies" (Schoultz 1998, 357). The Alliance for Progress was created to provide a stable model of development and social welfare to compete with Castro's revolutionary brand (Black 1988). However, from the start, this "was a two-pronged strategy: it sought to undercut support for the Left through economic development, while using military methods to suppress guerillas and other 'subversives.' The reforms petered out, but the military side of the Alliance endured" (Livingstone 2009, 40, emphasis in original). As part of the bureaucratic framework for the Alliance, the Agency for International Development (AID) was created to administer the American assistance programs. However, "by 1966 AID's police assistance bureau, the Office of Public Safety, was spending 38 percent of the entire economic assistance budget for Latin America to conduct counterinsurgency training in every country except Cuba" (Schoultz 1998, 359-360). Between 1964 and 1968, over 20,000 armed forces personnel from Latin America received training at the School of the Americas and other American military schools (Livingstone 2009). While the military to military relationships flourished, political support for the Alliance for Progress declined precipitously. Irritated at the perceived failure of the region to avail itself of American capital and guidance, by 1963 the "old attitudes about the slothfulness and incompetence of Latin American politicians were resurrected" (Black 1988, 114).

To stop a perceived drift towards the political Left in Brazil, the Johnson administration coordinated with that country's military to overthrow its democratically elected government in 1964 (Livingstone 2009). With strong public support, the United States invaded the Dominican Republic with 20,000 troops to prevent the reinstatement of its democratically elected president and demonstrate that it would not accept "another Cuba" in the region (Black 1988, 120). The Nixon administration worked diligently to prevent the election of socialist Salvador Allende as president of Chile in 1970 (Livingstone 2009). When that failed, the United States began a systematic effort to destabilize the country's economy while coordinating with the elements of the Chilean military that would overthrow and murder Allende in 1973 (Grow 2008). National Security Advisor Henry Kissinger's now infamous remarks in a White House meeting at the time voiced once again the predominant belief that Latin Americans – like children – had to be protected from themselves. "I don't see why we need to stand by and watch a country go Communist due to the irresponsibility of its own people" (quoted in Schoultz 1998, 361).

President Carter continued the practice of "uncritically accepting the hegemonic tradition of U.S. policy" (Ibid, 363). By the end of his term in office, the United States was sending millions of dollars in aid and military advisors to prop up the right-wing regime in El Salvador and funding efforts to destabilize the new leftist Sandinista government in Nicaragua (Cottam 1992; McPherson 2006). During the Reagan years, interest in human rights was jettisoned in favor of a strict Cold War ideology that viewed instability in Latin America – most notably the Caribbean region – as a test of America's global power and commitment by the Soviet bloc (Dominguez 1999). This commitment was demonstrated by the invasion of Grenada and the overthrow of its left leaning government in 1983 (Grow 2008). In a televised national address in 1984, President Reagan clearly outlined the nature of the perceived threat and the vehicle of its delivery. "Central America is a region of great importance to the United States. And it is so close – San Salvador is closer to Houston, Texas, than Houston is to Washington, D.C. Central America is America; *it's at our doorstep*. And it has become the stage for a bold attempt by the Soviet Union, Cuba, and Nicaragua to install communism by force throughout the hemisphere… What we see in El Salvador is an attempt to destabilize the entire region and eventually move chaos **and anarchy toward the American border**" (quoted in Holden and Zolov 2000, 295, emphasis added).

As in previous historical interactions, Latin America was viewed as both a natural extension of the United States – "at our doorstep" – and a potential source of infection (in this case, from communism) that endangered Americans. To stave off the threat of "chaos and anarchy" spreading to the United States, the Reagan administration financed the Contra insurgency inside Nicaragua, mined the country's harbors, and orchestrated a devastating international economic embargo (Livingstone

2009). Millions of dollars in military aid and advisors were channeled to El Salvador to support that government's fight against its leftist insurgency. Its open collusion with death squads and widespread use of torture had little impact on levels of financial assistance (McPherson 2006). Not simply a matter of national security, the Reagan administration publicly claimed that America's task was "to transform the crisis in Central America into an opportunity… and to use this to help our neighbors not only secure their freedom from aggression and violence, but also set in place the policies, processes, and institutions that will make them both prosperous and free" (Holden and Zolov 2000, 293-294). The states of Latin America required proper tutelage and could not be trusted to handle important matters on their own. Not surprisingly, indigenous local and regional efforts to resolve the conflicts in El Salvador and Nicaragua – at variance with American ideas and ideals – were "systematically opposed and undercut" by Washington (Dominguez 1999, 44).

The Drug War and Economic Integration

Although first promulgated under the Reagan administration, the Bush presidency made the newest contagion emanating from Latin America – the "drug threat" – the centerpiece of its post-Cold War regional strategy (Lehman 2006; Youngers and Rosin 2005). The process of "certification" (where the United States annually evaluated the drug control efforts of individual Latin American states), initiated under the Reagan administration, continued under Bush. "Governments that failed to meet these certification standards faced sanctions that included a cutoff of most forms of U.S. aid and trade benefits and, within multilateral lending institutions, an automatic 'no' vote by the influential U.S. representative on loan requests from the offending nation" (Isaacson 2005, 22). Seeing Latin America (and not domestic consumption) as the cause of America's drug woes, the Bush administration initiated the Andean Strategy – a highly militarized program designed to attack drug production on the ground in the source countries of Colombia, Peru, and Bolivia. Levels of military assistance to those states increased dramatically (Isaacson 2005; Loveman 2006). On the economic front, the "Washington consensus" (emphasizing deregulation, privatization, and exportation), was prescribed by the United States as the proper solution to Latin America's financial woes (McPherson 2006, 112).

The push for regional economic integration continued under the Clinton administration with the advent of the North American Free Trade Agreement (NAFTA) comprising Canada, Mexico, and the United States that went into effect in 1994 (Bulmer-Thomas and Page 1999). With Mexico generally perceived as "a low-wage, socially troubled, environmentally polluted country that exports illegal aliens to the United States" (Lewis and Ebrahim 1993, 829), the proposed high-level integration with this Latin republic initiated a national argument within the United States. While couched in the language of labor standards, environmental damage, and job growth or economic loss, central to this dispute were the historical representations of American superiority and Latin subordination. The positions of both sides were clearly represented in the November 9, 1993 debate on NAFTA between Vice President Al Gore (in support) and former presidential candidate Ross Perot (in opposition) televised on Cable News Network (CNN) (Rosenbaum 1993; Skonieczny 2001). As in the previous debates centering on increasing connection with Latin America, both sides agreed on the central premise of Mexico's essential inferiority and the exceptional nature of the United States. And, once again, advocates argued that America's exceptional nature would rehabilitate and renew Mexico while opponents maintained that Mexico would infect the United States and ruin that same exceptionalism (Lotz 1997; Skonieczny 2001). In the same year NAFTA went into effect, the Clinton administration sent troops into Haiti to ostensibly restore the deposed Aristide government. However, Aristide had been deposed and exiled in 1991 and neither the Bush nor the Clinton regimes had expressed interested in becoming involved (Coerver and Hall 1999). It was only when an exodus of Haitians refugees descending on Florida caused a domestic furor that Washington decided to act (Livingstone 2009). Consistent with historical patterns, instability in Latin America was expected but when it threatened American interests it would not be tolerated.

CONCLUSION

As demonstrated via the genealogical review from the 17th through the 20th centuries above, the Trump administration's discursive practices (attaching particular meanings to Latins, Latin America, and the United States) have long established antecedents that cannot be consigned to any single president, administration, or political party. Rather than an anomaly or aberration, the Trump immigration discourse is as American as apple pie. Latin Americans, due to the social and cultural baggage associated with mixed Iberian, African, and indigenous parentage, have been consistently characterized as uncivilized – trapped in the "state of nature" (Pike 1992). Conversely, the United States has been advanced as an exemplar of both external and internal development. This distinction – primitive/civilized and therefore subordinate/superior – served as a core logic or guiding opposition (Doty 1993) that functioned discursively to establish the terms (i.e., what was possible and what was not) of American policies towards the region.

This superior versus subordinate logic remains central to the Trump administration discourse on Latin immigrants and Latin America generally. In fact, this discourse cannot be intelligible without it. The United States instantiated in this discourse (regardless of any problems that require making it great *again*) could never be a "shithole" country like Haiti or El Salvador. Mexico, El Salvador, and Honduras are represented in the adminstration's discursive practices as out of control and impotent (Ackerman 2018; Meckler, Mauldin, and Pérez 2018). As constructed, these subjects are denied agency and positioned as second-rate countries. Conversely, the United States is brimming with agency. It has a "sacred border" (Youssef 2018b) and a military capable of fortifying it with an "impenetrable wall" (Caldwell 2018a; Wagner 2018). As the natural leader of the region dealing with inferiors (not democratic peers), the United

States instantiated in this discourse can call the shots and dictate terms (e.g., in terms of foreign aid, NAFTA, who will pay for the wall) (Ballhaus, Montes, and Pérez 2018; Corbett 2018; Meckler, Mauldin, and Pérez 2018).

As evidenced by this chapter's genealogy, the perception of Latin America's relative proximity to the borders of the United States – understood as being in its (back or front) "yard" or on its "doorstep" – cuts two ways. On the one hand, the region (most notably, its resources) is understood as a natural, commonsensical extension of the United States and thus, its proper domain (Kenworthy 1995; Schoultz 1998). On the other hand, the perpetual immediacy of Latin America serves as a continuous source of anxiety that some *contagion* (e.g., economic instability, communism, drugs, and/or refugees) emanating from the region will infect the United States (Black 1988). From Wilson and Mexico, through Reagan and Nicaragua to Clinton and Colombia, proximity has been a constant theme (Crandall 2002; Holden and Zolov 2000; Langley 1989). More recently, both President George W. Bush and President Barack Obama deployed the National Guard to assist with "border security" (Meckler, Gordon, and Caldwell 2018; Shoichet 2018) This historical "truth" remains central to the operating logic of the Trump discourse with its centerpiece of building a fortified wall. The proximity of the Mexican border (and all that is negatively envisioned beyond it) serves as a constant reminder that America must be vigilant, or it will be contaminated (or, in Trump speak, "stolen") (Ackerman and Meckler 2018). Within the pattern of tropes and predicates at play within this discursive activity, disparate Latin men, women, and children are denied individual identity and lumped together as thugs, drug dealers, rapists, gang members, and terrorists. The essential presupposition is that nothing good can come from or with these people from the South. To the Trump administration, they are an "onslaught" (Salama 2018) and an "invasion" (McDonnell 2018), constituting a "national emergency" (Montes 2018) that must be met with force (Salama 2018). In this vein, any deviation from a militarized strategy must rationally be characterized as a call for "open borders" and the surrender of the United States (Meckler, Gordon, and

Caldwell 2018). Therefore, the deployment of thousands of troops ("faithful patriots") to the border cannot be dismissed as a political stunt, but is rather, according to Defense Secretary Mattis, a logical response to the approaching migrant caravans. Mattis insists that this action is no different than the American military deployment in 1916 to guard against armed attacks from Mexico by the forces of Pancho Villa (Burns 2018; Youssef 2018b). It is this "common sense" of the inherent danger and threat emanating from these specific refugees that is central to the larger Trump immigration discourse but it *cannot be understood* outside the context of historical relations between the United States and Latin America.

REFERENCES

Ackerman, Andrew. 2018. "Trump Suggests Any DACA Deal with Democrats Is Dead; In Easter morning tweets, he also rebukes Mexico for 'doing very little, if not NOTHING' to stop immigrants crossing border." *Wall Street Journal*, April 1. Accessed December 30, 2018. https:// www.wsj.com/ articles/ trump-suggests-any-daca-deal-with-democrats-is-dead-1522607871.

Ackerman, Andrew, and Laura Meckler. 2018. "Donald Trump Says DACA Is Dead Because Democrats 'Didn't Care'; Continues calls via Twitter for tougher immigration laws, border wall." *Wall Street Journal*, April 2. Accessed December 30, 2018. https://www.wsj.com/ articles/donald-trump-says-daca-is-dead-because-democrats-dont-care-1522677860.

Ballhaus, Rebecca, Juan Montes, and Santiago Pérez. 2018. "Trump Threatens to Cut Off Aid to Honduras Over Immigration Caravan; Guatemalan authorities arrest Bartolo Fuentes, leader of the caravan of more than 1,500 migrants." *Wall Street Journal*, October 16. Accessed December 30, 2018. https://www.wsj.com/articles/trump-threatens-to-cut-off-aid-to-honduras-over-immigration-caravan-1539697747.

Black, George. 1988. *The good neighbor: how the United States wrote the history of Central America and the Caribbean*. 1st ed. New York: Pantheon Books.

Blake, Aaron. 2018. "Republicans swallowed the bait whole on Trump's terrorists-in-the-caravan innuendo." *The Washington Post*, November 19. Accessed December 30, 2018. https://www.washingtonpost.com/ politics/ 2018/ 11/ 19/ republicans-swallowed-bait-whole-trumps-terrorists-in-the-caravan-innuendo/?utm_term=.1c84389c1a46.

Brenner, Phillip, and Soraya Castro. 2009. "David and Gulliver: Fifty years of competing metaphors in the Cuban–United States relationship." *Diplomacy & Statecraft* 20 (2):236-257.

Bulmer-Thomas, V., and Sheila Page. 1999. "Trade, investment and NAFTA: The economics of neighbourhood." In *The United States and Latin America: the new agenda*, edited by V. Bulmer-Thomas and James Dunkerley, 75-98. London: Institute of Latin American Studies.

Burns, Robert. 2018. "Mattis compares border mission to one against Pancho Villa." *Daily Herald*, November 15. Accessed December 30, 2018. https://www.dailyherald.com/article/20181115/news/311159989.

Caldwell, Alicia A. 2018a. "Central American 'Caravan' Migrants to Seek Asylum at U.S.-Mexico Border; while many seek legal entry to U.S., some have already illegally crossed border." *Wall Street Journal*, April 29. Accessed December 30, 2018. https://www.wsj.com/articles/ central-american-caravan-migrants-to-seek-asylum-at-u-s-mexico-bord er-1524999600.

Caldwell, Alicia A. 2018b. "Immigrants Traveling as Families Arrested on Mexican Border Increase 38% in October; Nearly all have or will ask for asylum, U.S. officials say." *Wall Street Journal*, November 10. Accessed December 30, 2018. https://www.wsj.com/articles/ immigrants-traveling-as-families-arrested-on-mexican-border-increase-38-in-october-1541809167.

Campbell, David. 1998. *Writing security: United States foreign policy and the politics of identity*. Revised ed. Minneapolis: University of Minnesota.

Carabine, Jean. 2001. "Unmarried motherhood 1830-1990: A genealogical analysis." In *Discourse as data: a guide for analysis*, edited by Simeon Yates, Stephanie Taylor and Margaret Wetherell. London; Thousand Oaks, Calif: SAGE.

Coerver, Don M., and Linda B. Hall. 1999. *Tangled destinies: Latin America and the United States*. 1st ed, *Diálogos*. Albuquerque: University of New Mexico Press.

Collinson, Stephen, and Jeremy Diamond. 2016. *Trump finally admits it: 'President Barack Obama was born in the United States'*. CNN.com, Last Modified September 16, 2016, accessed December 20, 2018. https://www.cnn.com/2016/09/15/politics/donald-trump-obama-birther-united-states/index.html.

Corbett, Erin. 2018. *Trump Has Said Mexico Will Pay for the Border Wall at Least 20 Times Since 2015*. Fortune.com, Last Modified December 13, 2018, accessed December 30, 2018. http://fortune.com/2018/12/13/trump-mexico-border-wall/.

Cortes, Steve. 2018. *Trump's Approval Rating Rises Among Hispanics*. Real Clear Politics, Last Modified June 29, 2018, accessed December 30, 2018. https://www.realclearpolitics.com/articles/2018/06/28/trumps_approval_rating_rises_among_hispanics_137382.html.

Cottam, Martha L. 1992. "The Carter administration's policy toward Nicaragua: images, goals, and tactics." *Political Science Quarterly* 107 (1):123-146.

Dawsey, Josh. 2018. "Trump derides protections for immigrants from 'shithole' countries." *The Washington Post*, January 12. Accessed December 30, 2018. https://www.washingtonpost.com/politics/trump-attacks-protections-for-immigrants-from-shithole-countries-in-oval-office-meeting/2018/01/11/bfc0725c-f711-11e7-91af-31ac729add94_story.html?noredirect=on&utm_term=.9787441dca36.

deCordoba, Jose, and Robbie Whelan. 2018. "Migrant 'Caravan' in Mexico Raises Trump's Ire; Annual protest march to U.S. border prompts tweets criticizing Mexico, DACA, and NAFTA." *Wall Street Journal (Online)*, April 2. Accessed December 30, 2018. https://www.

wsj.com/articles/migrant-caravan-in-mexico-raises-trumps-ire-152270
8047.

Dominguez, Jorge I. 1999. "US-Latin American relations during the Cold War and its aftermath." In *The United States and Latin America: the new agenda*, edited by V. Bulmer-Thomas and James Dunkerley, 33-50. London: Institute of Latin American Studies.

Epstein, Charlotte. 2008. *The power of words in international relations: birth of an anti-whaling discourse*. Cambridge, Mass.: MIT Press.

Fairclough, Norman. 1998. "Political discourse in the media: An analytical framework." In *Approaches to media discourse*, edited by Allan Bell and Peter Garrett, 142-152. Oxford; Malden, Mass.: Blackwell.

Grow, Michael. 2008. *U.S. presidents and Latin American interventions: pursuing regime change in the Cold War*. Lawrence, Kan.: University Press of Kansas.

Halle, Louis (aka "Y"). 1950. "On a Certain Impatience with Latin America." *Foreign Affairs* 28 (July):565-579.

Hansen, Allen Dreyer, and Eva Sørensen. 2005. "Polity as politics: studying the shaping and effects of discursive polities." In *Discourse theory in European politics: identity, policy, and governance*, edited by David R. Howarth and Jacob Torfing, 93-116. Basingstoke, Hampshire; New York: Palgrave Macmillan.

Holden, Robert H., and Eric Zolov. 2000. *Latin America and the United States: a documentary history*. New York: Oxford University Press.

Holloway, Johnny. 2012. *Superiority and Subordination in U.S. – Latin America Relations: A Discourse Analysis of Plan Colombia*. PhD Dissertation, School of International Service, American University.

Horsman, Reginald. 1998. "Liberty and the Anglo-Saxons." In *Race and U.S. foreign policy from colonial times through the age of Jackson*, edited by Michael L. Krenn, 99-120. New York: Garland Pub.

Howarth, David R. 2000. *Discourse, Concepts in the social sciences*. Buckingham England; Philadelphia, PA: Open University Press.

Howarth, David R., and Jacob Torfing. 2005. *Discourse theory in European politics: identity, policy, and governance*. Houndmills, Basingstoke, Hampshire; New York: Palgrave Macmillan.

Hunt, Michael H. 1987. *Ideology and U.S. foreign policy*. New Haven: Yale University Press.

Isaacson, Adam. 2005. "The U.S. military in the War on Drugs." In *Drugs and democracy in Latin America: the impact of U.S. policy*, edited by Coletta Youngers and Eileen Rosin, 15-60. Boulder, Colo.: L. Rienner.

Jackson, Patrick T. 2006. *Civilizing the enemy: German reconstruction and the invention of the West*. Ann Arbor: University of Michigan Press.

Johnson, John J. 1980. *Latin America in caricature*. Austin: University of Texas Press.

Johnson, John J. 1990. *A hemisphere apart: the foundations of United States policy toward Latin America*. Baltimore: Johns Hopkins University Press.

Jørgensen, Marianne, and Louise Phillips. 2002. *Discourse analysis as theory and method*. London; Thousand Oaks, Calif.: Sage Publications.

Keen, Benjamin. 1969. "The Black Legend revisited: Assumptions and realities." *Hispanic American Historical Review* 49 (4):703-719.

Kenworthy, Eldon. 1995. *America/Américas: myth in the making of U.S. policy toward Latin America*. University Park, Pa.: Pennsylvania State University Press.

Krenn, Michael L. 2006. *The color of empire: race and American foreign relations*. 1st ed. Washington, D.C.: Potomac Books.

Krogstad, Jens Manuel, Antonio Flores, and Mark Hugo Lopez. 2018. *Key takeaways about Latino voters in the 2018 midterm elections*. Pew Research Center, Last Modified November 9, 2018, accessed December 30, 2018. http://www.pewresearch.org/fact-tank/2018/11/09/how-latinos-voted-in-2018-midterms/.

Krotofil, Joanna, and Dominika Motak. 2018. "A critical discourse analysis of the media coverage of the migration crisis in Poland: The Polish Catholic Church's perception of the 'migration crisis'." *Scripta Instituti Donneriani Aboensis* 28:92-115.

Langley, Lester D. 1989. *America and the Americas: the United States in the Western Hemisphere*. Athens: University of Georgia Press.

Langley, Lester D. 2010. *America and the Americas: the United States in the Western Hemisphere*. 2nd ed. Athens: University of Georgia Press.

Leary, Alex. 2018. "Trump Aims to Fire Up Republican Voters Over Immigration; So far, GOP candidates' ads don't emphasize issue, and Democrats say it alienates independents." *Wall Street Journal*, October 18. Accessed December 30, 2018. https://www.wsj.com/articles/trump -aims-to-fire-up-republican-voters-over-immigration-1539906051.

Lee, Michelle Ye Hee. 2015. "Donald Trump's false comments connecting Mexican immigrants and crime." *The Washington Post*, July 8. Accessed December 30, 2018. https://www.washingtonpost.com/ news/ fact-checker/ wp/ 2015/ 07/ 08/ donald-trumps-false-comments-connecting-mexican-immigrants-and-crime/?noredirect=on&utm_term =.f15a872e4641.

Lehman, Kenneth. 2006. "A medicine of "death"? U.S. policy and political disarray in Bolivia, 1985-2006." In *Addicted to failure: U.S. security policy in Latin America and the Andean Region*, edited by Brian Loveman, 130-168. Lanham, Md.: Rowman & Littlefield Publishers.

Lewis, Charles, and Margaret Ebrahim. 1993. "Can Mexico and Big Business USA buy NAFTA?" *The Nation*, 826-839.

Linthicum, Kate. 2018. "Pueblo Sin Fronteras uses caravans to shine light on the plight of migrants — but has that backfired?" *Los Angeles Times*, December 6. Accessed December 30, 2018. https://www.latime s.com/world/mexico-americas/la-fg-mexico-caravan-leaders-20181206 -story.html.

Livingstone, Grace. 2009. *America's backyard: the United States and Latin America from the Monroe Doctrine to the War on Terror*. London; New York: Zed Books.

Lotz, Hellmut. 1997. "Myth and NAFTA: The use of core values in US politics." In *Culture & foreign policy*, edited by Valerie M. Hudson, 73-96. Boulder, Colo.: L. Rienner Publishers.

Loveman, Brian. 2006. "U.S. security policies in Latin America and the Andean Region, 1990-2006." In *Addicted to failure: U.S. security policy in Latin America and the Andean Region*, edited by Brian Loveman, 1-52. Lanham, Md.: Rowman & Littlefield Publishers.

McDonnell, Patrick J. 2018. "Trump's border wall, long an incendiary issue, hasn't come up in talks with U.S., new Mexican leader says."

Los Angeles Times, December 13. Accessed December 30, 2018. https:// www.latimes.com/ world/ mexico-americas/ la-fg-mexico-wall-20181213-story.html.

McDougall, Walter A. 1997. *Promised land, crusader state: the American encounter with the world since 1776*. Boston: Houghton Mifflin.

McPherson, Alan L. 2006. *Intimate ties, bitter struggles: the United States and Latin America since 1945*. 1st ed. Washington, D.C.: Potomac Books.

Meckler, Laura, Lubold Gordon, and Alicia A. Caldwell. 2018. "Trump Administration Unveils Plans to Send National Guard Troops, Build Base Walls Near U.S.-Mexico Border; Homeland Security secretary says agency and Pentagon will be directed to work with governors on deployment." *Wall Street Journal*, April 4. Accessed December 30, 2018. https://www.wsj.com/articles/trump-to-sign-proclamation-sending-national-guard-troops-to-border-regions-1522871401.

Meckler, Laura, William Mauldin, and Santiago Pérez. 2018. "Donald Trump Calls for Military to Guard Southern Border; President suggests he might use Nafta talks to pressure Mexico to halt protest march of asylum seekers from Central America." *Wall Street Journal*, April 3. Accessed December 30, 2018. https://www.wsj.com/articles/trump-threatens-nafta-honduras-aid-over-migrant-caravan-1522763515.

Milliken, Jennifer. 1999. "The Study of Discourse in International Relations: A Critique of Research and Methods." *European Journal of International Relations* 5 (2):225-254.

Montes, Juan. 2018. "Caravan Heads North After Migrants Cross Into Mexico; The caravan of migrants could fuel a fresh political rift between Trump and Mexico two weeks before U.S. midterm elections." *Wall Street Journal*, October 22. Accessed December 30, 2018. https://www.wsj.com/articles/caravan-heads-north-after-migrants-cross-into-mexico-1540143333.

Montoya-Galvez, Camilo. 2019. *"DHS to ask Pentagon for more troops on the border."* CBS News, Last Modified January 3, 2019, accessed January 3, 2019. https://www.cbsnews.com/news/department-of-homeland-security-to-ask-pentagon-for-more-troops-on-the-border/.

Ninkovich, Frank A. 2001. *The United States and imperialism*. Malden, Mass.: Blackwell Publishers.

Obeidallah, Dean. 2018. *Trump is trying to whip up fear about the browning of America*. CNN.com, Last Modified November 4, 2018, accessed December 30, 2018. https://www.cnn.com/2018/11/04/opinions/trump-whip-up-browning-of-america-obeidallah/index.html.

Oliphant, Baxter. 2018. *After 17 years of war in Afghanistan, more say U.S. has failed than succeeded in achieving its goals*. Pew Research Center, Last Modified October 5, 2018, accessed December 30, 2018. http://www.pewresearch.org/ fact-tank/ 2018/ 10/ 05/ after-17-years-of-war-in-afghanistan-more-say-u-s-has-failed-than-succeeded-in-achieving-its-goals/.

Parker, Ashley, and Steve Edar. 2016. "Inside the Six Weeks Donald Trump was a Nonstop 'Birther'." *The New York Times*, July 2. Accessed December 28, 2018. https://www.nytimes.com/2016/07/03/us/politics/donald-trump-birther-obama.html?module=inline.

Pérez, Louis A. 2008. *Cuba in the American imagination: metaphor and the imperial ethos*. Chapel Hill: University of North Carolina Press.

Phillips, Nelson, and Cynthia Hardy. 2002. *Discourse analysis: investigating processes of social construction, Qualitative research methods; v. 50*. Thousand Oaks, CA: Sage Publications.

Pike, Fredrick B. 1992. *The United States and Latin America: myths and stereotypes of civilization and nature*. 1st ed. Austin: University of Texas Press.

Reisigl, Martin, and Ruth Wodak. 2001. *Discourse and discrimination: rhetorics of racism and antisemitism*. London; New York: Routledge.

Richards, Kimberley. 2018. "Ocasio-Cortez Says Claire McCaskill Calling Her A 'Shiny Object' To CNN Is 'Disappointing': The outgoing senator once warned Democrats not to go "so far to the left"." *HuffPost*, Last Modified December 29, 2018, accessed December 30, 2018. https://www.huffingtonpost.com/entry/alexandria-ocasio-cortez-claire-mccaskill-shiny-object_us_5c27f909e4b05c88b700f9da.

Rizzo, Salvador. 2018. "Fact-checking Trump's weekly address on immigrants, crime and sanctuary cities." *The Washington Post*, March

15. Accessed December 30, 2018. https://www.washingtonpost.com/ news/fact-checker/wp/2018/03/15/fact-checking-trumps-weekly-addres s-on-immigrants-crime-and-sanctuary-cities/?utm_term=.8b8aaf79565 7.

Rosenbaum, David E. 1993. "The Vice President accuses foe of taking stance for personal gain." *New York Times*, November 10, A1; B15.

Salama, Vivian. 2018. "Trump Threatens to 'Call Up the U.S. Military' If Mexico Doesn't Stop Migrants; President asks southern neighbor to 'stop the onslaught' of Latin American migrants heading to U.S." *Wall Street Journal*, October 18. Accessed December 30, 2018. https:// www.wsj.com/articles/trump-threatens-to-call-up-the-u-s-military-if-m exico-doesnt-stop-migrants-1539866223.

Schneider, Jessica, Geneva Sands, and David Shortell. 2018. *Counterterrorism official contradicts Trump: No sign ISIS or 'Sunni terrorist groups' are in caravan.* CNN.com, Last Modified October 22, 2018, accessed December 30, 2018. https://www.cnn.com/2018/10/ 22/politics/caravan-terrorism-trump/index.html.

Schoultz, Lars. 1998. *Beneath the United States: a history of U.S. policy toward Latin America.* Cambridge, Mass.: Harvard University Press.

Shear, Michael D., and Julie Hirschfeld Davis. 2018. "As Midterm Vote Nears, Trump Reprises a Favorite Message: Fear Immigrants." *The New York Times*, November 1. Accessed December 30, 2018. https:// www.nytimes.com/2018/11/01/us/politics/trump-immigration.html.

Shoichet, Catherine E. 2018. *Trump says he'll send the military to the border. Bush and Obama did, too.* CNN.com, Last Modified April 4, 2018, accessed December 30, 2018. https://www.cnn.com/2018/04/03/ politics/border-troops-deployed-obama-bush/index.html.

Skonieczny, Amy. 2001. "Constructing NAFTA: Myth, representation, and the discursive construction of U.S. foreign policy." *International Studies Quarterly* 45 (3):433-454.

Smith, Joseph. 2005. *The United States and Latin America: a history of American diplomacy, 1776-2000.* London; New York: Routledge.

Stillar, Glenn F. 1998. Analyzing everyday texts: discourse, rhetoric, and social perspectives. *Rhetoric & society*. Thousand Oaks, Calif: Sage Publications.

Taylor, Stephanie. 2001. "Locating and conducting discourse analytic research." In *Discourse as data: a guide for analysis*, edited by Simeon Yates, Stephanie Taylor and Margaret Wetherell, 5-48. London; Thousand Oaks, Calif: SAGE.

Time Staff. 2015. *Here's Donald Trump's Presidential Announcement Speech*. Time, Last Modified June 16. http://time.com/3923128/donald-trump-announcement-speech/.

Torfing, Jacob. 2005. "Discourse theory: Achievements, arguments and challenges." In *Discourse theory in European politics: identity, policy, and governance*, edited by David R. Howarth and Jacob Torfing, 1-30. Houndmills, Basingstoke, Hampshire; New York: Palgrave Macmillan.

Wagner, John. 2018. "Across five tweets, Trump makes a meandering case for border wall funding." *The Washington Post*, December 11, 2018. Accessed December 29, 2018. https://www.washingtonpost.com/politics/across-five-tweets-trump-makes-a-meandering-case-for-border-wall-funding/2018/12/11/8ea6ad64-fd35-11e8-862a-b6a6f3ce8199_story.html?utm_term=.deb5dff9cfe6.

Weston, Rubin F. 1998. "Racism and the Imperialist Campaign." In *Race and U.S. foreign policy in the ages of territorial and market expansion, 1840 to 1900*, edited by Michael L. Krenn, 189-207. New York: Garland Pub.

Wolf, Z. Byron. 2017. *Read this: How Trump defended criticism of judge for being 'Mexican'*. CNN.com, Last Modified April 20, 2017, accessed December 29, 2018. https://www.cnn.com/2017/04/20/politics/donald-trump-gonzalo-curiel-jake-tapper-transcript/index.html.

Youngers, Coletta, and Eileen Rosin. 2005. "The U.S. 'War on Drugs': Its impact in Latin America and the Caribbean." In *Drugs and democracy in Latin America: the impact of U.S. policy*, edited by Coletta Youngers and Eileen Rosin, 1-14. Boulder, Colo.: L. Rienner.

Youssef, Nancy A. 2018a. "Troops Deploy to Parts of Border Where Migrant Caravans Are Deemed Most Likely to Go; More than 3,500

U.S. troops have been deployed near three areas of California, Texas and Arizona where it would be safer and easier for migrants to cross into the U.S." *Wall Street Journal*, November 3. Accessed December 30, 2018. https://www.wsj.com/articles/troops-deploy-to-parts-of-bord er-where-migrant-caravans-are-deemed-most-likely-to-go-1541160003

Youssef, Nancy A. 2018b. "Trump Calls for Up to 15,000 Troops at Border as Election Nears; President reprises attack on birthright citizenship; defense chief rejects critics who say deployment is aimed to help GOP." *Wall Street Journal*, October 31. Accessed December 30, 2018. https://www.wsj.com/articles/mattis-defends-troop-deployment-to-mexican-border-1541015382.

Zhou, Li. 2018. *9 experts warn that Latino dislike of Trump may not translate into midterm turnout: It really comes down to whether Democrats invest in voter outreach.* Vox.com, Last Modified October 22, 2018, accessed December 30, 2018. https://www.vox.com/policy-and-politics/ 2018/ 9/ 19/17851934/hispanic-latino-voters-trump-polls-turnout.

Zurcher, Anthony. 2018. "The one Trump statistic that explains everything." *BBC News*, Last Modified June 5, 2018, accessed December 30, 2018. https://www.bbc.com/news/world-us-canada-44324545.

In: A Closer Look at Political Communication   ISBN: 978-1-53615-321-7
Editor: Mark H. Tatum   © 2019 Nova Science Publishers, Inc.

Chapter 4

THE POWER OF POLITICAL PRAYER IN NIGERIA

Ibrahim S. Bitrus[1,], PhD*

[1]Department of Systematic Theology,
Bronnum Lutheran Seminary, Yola, Adamawa, Nigeria

ABSTRACT

Prayer has traditionally been used in Christianity as a spiritual means to commune with God, but also to beseech God to address the felt needs and fears of the petitioners. But prayer has lately been used in the church by many Nigerian politicians for personal gain. In particular, politicians have deployed prayer as a campaign tool to mobile the church to support the struggle for achieving their political ambitions. In this article I explore this phenomenon of politicians employing prayer in the church as a potent political tool to subtly campaign for election and reelection in Nigeria. I would argue that the phenomenon of seeking political power through prayer by politicians confers reciprocal political power on both the politicians and the clergy alike.

---

* Corresponding Author Email: bitrus_ibrahim@yahoo.com.

INTRODUCTION

Politics is largely seen in Nigeria as a "dirty" game, which defiles Christians who get involved in the game. This is because it is usually characterized by thuggery, rigging, betrayal, vendetta, false promises and violence. Those who engage in politics are viewed as participating in a dirty business. Many Nigerian politicians therefore lack public trust and confidence. Associating prayer with politics will appear to many Christians as an unholy and unspiritual alliance. But as we shall see in this chapter, political leadership is ordained by God for the common good of the society. There is a significant holy relationship between prayer and the quest for political power in the church. Thus, politicians who express the genuine desire to run for political leadership in the Church of God are expressing a godly, honorable, and noble desire in the sight of God.

What this means is that Christians who participate in politics are not simply participating in human, but God's business. God who establishes political leadership desires faithful and godly people to occupy it. In many ways, it is contrary to God's loving will for villains and tyrants to occupy leadership positions to the detriment of our collective good. Therefore, there is nothing "dirty" about godly Christians vying for political leadership and asking the church to give them every necessary moral and prayerful support it takes for them to realize their political ambitions. In this essay, I will unearth the significant spiritual relationship that exists between prayer and political power. I will explore the phenomenon of politicians using prayer in the church as a campaign tool for capturing state leadership and resources.

CAMPAIGN IN THE NAME OF PRAYER

Nigeria is a democratic country which one of its essential features is holding of a periodic election. The Nigerian periodic general elections are scheduled for February 2019. In these forthcoming elections, Nigerians will go to the pool to exercise their right to vote. They will participate in the elections of the president, Vice President, members of the National Assembly, governors, their deputies and the members of the houses of assembly. Those running for these public offices are employing a myriad of campaign strategies to woo the support of the Nigerian electorate, but also to defeat their political opponents whether they are fellow contestants or those who seek to frustrate their political dreams.

To gain the vote of the people, politicians would usually deploy rather soft, nonaggressive, and persuasive campaign strategies. First, they hold political rallies where they would make promises to the electorate. As a developing nation that exhibits every index of underdevelopment, politicians would promise to fight endemic corruption, insecurity, poverty, joblessness, dilapidated social infrastructures such as bad roads, inadequate teaching-learning facilities and aids, poor healthcare delivery, and insufficient safe drinking water. President Muhammadu Buhari's 2015 campaign promises for example, centered on these national issues. Like any other politicians he proclaims to the people that if elected he would run an incorruptible government, protect life and property, create wealth and jobs and fix the broken basic social infrastructures to improve their living standards. One of the promises Buhari made on politics and governance was to "initiate action to amend the Nigerian Constitution with a view to devolving powers, duties, and responsibilities to states in order to entrench true Federalism and the Federal spirit." On national security and defense, he says he would "urgently address capacity building mechanisms of law enforcement agents in terms of quantity and quality as this is critical in safeguarding the sanctity of lives and property."[1]

In addition to rallies, political candidates use political advertisement campaign strategy to influence the voting behavior of the electorates in their favor. Grace Izeghe Ojekwe argues that though political campaign adverts make an insignificant impact on electorates' voting behavior, they play a role in the overall political campaign process. Ojekwe writes, "Political parties and their candidates are becoming increasingly aware of

---

[1] "What Buhari Promised Nigerians," *Vanguard,* May 28, 2015, https://www.vanguardngr. com/2015/05/what-buhari-promised-nigerians/ (accessed July 25, 2018).

the effectiveness of advertising and its role in getting the electorates to choose a particular candidate or party over the other by way of informing them. The use of political ad campaigns. . . bridges the communication gap between political parties, political candidates and electorates."[2] Thus, political aspirants set aside significant percent of their campaign budgets for political adverts. They deploy print and electronic media the most effective of which are radio, television, newspapers, billboard, and social media to advertise themselves and their campaign promises. Past and current political aspirants would float these traditional and modern media with persuasive political manifestos and jingles which express the compendium of their campaign promises to the general public.

Political candidates use the media not only positively to boost their credentials and publicize their manifestos, they also use it to launch vicious attack against their opponents. Isaac Olawale Albert argues, "Such [negative] campaigns are usually bereft of issues and often slide into mudslinging or smear campaigns in which the candidate who has been attacked launches his or her own negative campaign."[3] In the 2015 presidential election, the ruling party at the time, PDP sponsored television programs that discredited health status and the academic qualification of General Muhammadu Buhari, the presidential aspirant of the opposition party, APC. In turn, Buhari portrayed his rival, president Goodluck Jonathan the PDP presidential aspirant as a clueless, weak, and incompetent leader, who has failed to secure the life and property of Nigerians against the onslaught of Boko Haram. Daniel Ofomegbe Ekhareafo and Isaac Michael Akoseogasimhe get it right in their research, "The 2015 presidential election campaigns were overshadowed by prevailing negative tactics, with escalating mutual accusations and fierce

---

[2] Grace Izeghe Ojekwe, "*Political Advert Campaigns and Voting Behaviour: A Study of Akinwunmi Ambode's Election Ad Campaigns in Lagos State*," http://www.inec nigeria.org/wp-content/uploads/2015/07/Conference-Paper-by-Grace-Ojekwe.pdf (accessed August 3, 2018).

[3] Isaac Olawale Albert, "A Review of the Campaign Strategies," in *Journal of African Elections* 6, no. 2 (2007): 59.

personal attacks. The inflammatory language and hate speech were increasingly used in the campaign."[4]

When conventional campaign promises, and political advert fail elicit the support of the public they need to win elective office, political candidates and parties resort to unconventional means such as explicit vote buying and political intimidation to achieve their political ambitions. They often do this by offering money and other material goods to the electorate in return for people's vote. Micheal Bratton argues that the strategy of vote buying and political intimidation, which coerces electorate into voting candidates, is a crucial aspect of Nigerian election campaigns. According to him "fewer than one out of five Nigerians is personally exposed to vote buying and fewer than one in ten experiences threats of electoral violence."[5]

But virtually none of these "secular" campaign strategies are practicable for politicians to deploy in the church. They would instead adopt rather a "sacred" campaign strategy to mobilize the support of the church for their political aspirations. This sacred strategy is prayer, a spiritual tool used in the church to achieve a mundane desire. Political candidates almost always employ prayer, a solemn, but dynamic powerful spiritual resource in their pursuit of political office in the Church of God. The phenomenon of politicians campaigning for votes in the Church under the pretext of seeking prayer for their election/re-election is pervasive in Nigeria. In fact, it upsurges whenever elections are drawing nearer. During elections season politicians avail themselves of every opportunity to visit churches to lobby them for prayerful support. Samuel Ekekere accurately writes, "politicians are using churches as campaign grounds as they move from Sunday to Sunday to different church meet[ings] in a bid to arouse

---

[4] Daniel Ofomegbe Ekhareafo and Isaac Michael Akoseogasimhe, "A Textual Analysis of 2015 Presidential Election Advertisements in Selected Nigerian Newspapers," *MCC* 1, no. 1 (2017):168.

[5] Micheal Bratton, "Voting Buying and Violence in Nigerian Election Campaigns," in *Afrobarometer,* (2008): 15. https://www.files.ethz.ch/isn/91313/AfropaperNo99.pdf (accessed August 19, 2018).

interest from church followers."[6] They visit with churches to request pastors to pray for them, to invoke their blessing ahead of elections, and to have some of the pastors prophesied to them the good news of electoral victory regardless of whether the prophecy will come to fulfillment or not. When politicians seeking election/re-election ask the church to pray for them, they are "simply asking the church to vote for them."[7] This type of prayer is what I call "political prayer." It is the prayer offered to God by the church for political leaders and aspirants seeking divine power and support of the church to capture and maintain grip on state power and resources.

For instance, during the 2011 pre-general elections season president Jonathan who was running for re-election at the time visited the convention grounds of the Redeemed Christian Church of God (RCCG) on the Lagos-Ibadan Expressway, where the General Overseer, Pastor Enoch Adejare Adeboye prayed for him while kneeling in front the Overseer. According to Sahara Reporters, "On that occasion, President Jonathan was also allowed to speak, which was the equivalent of a campaign opportunity, if not outright endorsement. He appropriately thanked the General Overseer and members of the Church for giving him to the privilege."[8] He also visited with Living Faith Church, one of the leading Nigerian Pentecostal churches, ahead of the 2015 general elections. Jonathan, who told the worshipers that he was not attending the church service to campaign, appealed to them to pray for the forthcoming general elections. After the speech, Bishop David Oyedepo asked the members to stand up and pray for the president. The church prayed God to endow the president with wisdom, grace and strength to lead the country with the fear of God.[9]

---

[6] Samuel Okekere, "Why Nigerian Pastors Should Stop Allowing Politicians to Campaign Inside Churches," *NaijaGists.com*, https://naijagists.com/why-nigerian-pastors-should-stop-allowing-politicians-to-campaign-inside-churches/ (accessed August 14, 2018).

[7] Interview with Rev Benedict Barde Cham, August 19, 2018.

[8] "Election: Pastor Bakare Challenges Christian Church Over Political Support, Alleges Some Pastors Sold Their Conscience In 2011," *Sahara Reporters,* http://saharareporters.com/2015/01/06/election-pastor-bakare-challenges-christian-church-over-political-support-alleges-some (accessed August 15, 2015).

[9] See Oge Okonkwo, "Members of Popular Church 'Divided' over Jonathan's Visit," *Purse*, https://www.pulse.ng/communities/religion/winners-chapel-members-of-popular-church-divided-over-jonathans-visit-id3438602.html (accessed August 15, 2018).

The current governor of Adamawa state, senator Muhammad Jibrilla Bindow, a Muslim while running for the governorship of the state in 2015 visited the convention grounds of the Lutheran Church of Christ in Nigeria, LCCN. He asked the church to pray for him. He said the Spirit has laid on his heart to build the convention center if elected as the governor of the state. Another Muslim, Alhaji Ahmed Nwagubi, the House Representative candidate, visited Bonotem diocese convention center in 2010 to solicit prayer from the church. I was one of the guest speakers at this Lutheran convention. Nwagubi was exceedingly wise and enthralling about the way he presented his prayer request for vying for political leadership to the large gathering of the Lutheran conventioneers. He grounded his political prayer request in the Bible, quoting Matthew 7:7-8, which he claimed to be his most favorite verse of the Bible.

> Ask, and it will be given you; search, and you will find; knock, and the door will be opened for you. For everyone who asks receives, and everyone who searches finds, and for everyone who knocks, the door will be opened.[10]

Quite lately this year, governor Ishaku Darius of Taraba State, who is running for re-election, attended the 50th birthday celebration of my Rev Philip Micah Dopah in the United Methodist Church of Nigeria (UMCN), Jalingo. I was quest preacher. Darius praised the celebrant for being a man of integrity, peace, and a champion of social justice. He apologized for his inability to resolve the lingering crisis of the church. "If the warring leaders of the church should decide to part ways," he advised they should do so in good faith and in peace. He highlighted the monumental achievements of his administration and promised to consolidate them if re-elected. He concluded his speech by asking the church to pray for him and his transformative political agenda for the state. In response, the celebrant, who is the leader of the Southern conference of the UMCN, thanked the governor for assisting the church and assured him of his church continued prayer and support. A political prayer was said for the governor. The

---

[10] Matthew 7:7-8. NRSV.

incidences of politicians visiting with churches across Nigeria to seek prayer for seizing political power are rather inexhaustible to explore in this essay.

But one may wonder why Church leaders insist on praying for political aspirants seeking power even though they know that these politicians are campaigning for vote under the cover of prayer request in the church. Why shouldn't they decline to pray? Rev Cham who has before offered such a political prayer for politicians says that the church leaders would not often decline to participate in political prayer for two reasons. The first reason is that church leaders consider prayer request from political candidates to be an opportunity for them to articulate the religious and social concerns and programs of the church community, which they would demand these candidates to make public commitments to addressing and implementing them if elected/re-elected. An opportunity like this where the church leaders advocate for social and political changes in the church and society to politicians is rare and church leaders can't afford to reject it. They would always want to take advantage of that. The other reason is that political prayer for politicians is often accompanied by a "large package of gift" for the church leaders.[11] The package often contains enormous sum of money that runs in millions, though the amount varies from one candidate to the other. This underscores the reason for Nigerian church leaders to also invite political aspirants to visit their places of worship and convention centers for prayer during the season of political campaign. Often times politicians would gladly honor such an invite and would not let it escape them by all means. The invite is usually a long-awaited opportunity for them to campaign, but also to seek God's favor and protection in the church.

In Nigeria where politics is seen as a "war," in which most politicians use all means and forces, including evil ones to eliminate their opponents in their quest to capture state power, political candidates need this divine protection. They need God to protect them from these vicious political opponents and mysterious powers such as secret cults and witches that

---

[11] Interview with Cham.

their political enemies may deploy to destroy them during campaign. There is no better place to look for this protection than in the church. This is because the practice of Nigerian politicians spending reasonable financial resources on obtaining supernatural protection against political opponents from unchristian resource persons other than pastors during election is not uncommon. Politicians, according to Patrick Wilmot, spent fortunes during election "on mallams, medicine men, and witch doctors to provide [them] with mystical protection or the power to destroy opponents."[12] Thus, church leaders pray for politicians in the church during election not just for them to win the election, but also to assure them of God's protection over their lives against the destructive powers of their political rivals. The truth is that it is better ethically for the politicians to spend their time and resources on consulting with the church and its pastors than seeking help from unchristian sources in their quest for divine protection.

At any rate, it is very clear from the foregoing that prayer is so profoundly essential for politicians to enlist God's protection and support of the Church in the pursuit of state power and resources. Prayer and pursuit of political leadership are interwoven. Again, the Church is a crucial neutral sacred public sphere for politicians of diverse backgrounds to pursue their legitimate political desires under the pretext of prayer request. I will come back to this later.

THE POWER OF PUBLIC PRAYER

Prayer is not a redundant human exercise. It is a spiritual exercise that impacts our world. Prayer changes life and circumstances for better when it is grounded in God as its primary agent who imparts the change. It is a powerful resource for spiritual and social transformation. It is not simply a spiritual tool deployed by Christians for inner personal peace, solace and deliverance in times of conflict and trouble. Prayer, according to Tobin Miller Shearer, is a "dynamic ritual that generates social change rather than

---

[12] Patrick F. Wilmot, *Sociology: A New Introduction* (London: Collins International Textbooks, 1985), 140.

static words that mark identity, and foe means through which political action is taken, not a state-protected tool of personal salvation."[13] Shearer explores the use of Christian public prayer in the U.S. during the civil rights movement. He concludes that prayer was used not only to address pressing political issues and draw public attention. The civil rights activists used it also as a powerful resource in the pursuit of racial justice and equity.

Prayer is a divine means to unsettle the status quo of unjust social structures and oppression and to usher in new public order characterized by justice, rule of law, and equity. It is a rebellion against evil forces that disrupt and impede the enjoyment of God's provision of abundant life in the world. Prayer is a resistance resource that Jesus himself used. According to Jan Schnell Rippentrop, Jesus deployed prayer to encourage the disciples to action: "Get up, let us be going" (14:42). Rippentrop writes, "Through prayer, one can listen and discern so that one's participation in social transformation remains consistent with God's mission in the world. With the positive resistance that prayer offers, Christians can remain committed to God's ways in the world and be ready to 'get up and be going' when action is needed."[14]

But prayer is also used to legitimize structures of injustice and oppression rather than destabilizing it.[15] In this sense, it is a weapon to subvert social and political change that may bring about freedom, liberation, and social justice. Whenever there is any conflict between the prayer which seeks to overturn the status quo and the one that seeks to maintain it, then the prayer that says, "thy will be done" takes precedence over all of them.[16]

Accordingly, prayer is more than what we do. It is what God does in and through us in the Spirit in conformity with God's will. "The Spirit

---

[13] Tobin Miller Shearer, "Invoking Crisis: Performative Christian Prayer and the Civil Rights Movement," in *Journal of the American Academy of Religion* 83, no 2 (2015): 490.

[14] Jan Schnell Rippentrop, "Marks Passion Narrative as Political Theology," *Currents in Theology and Mission* 44, no. 4 (2017): 17. 11-19. https://content.ebscohost.com/ContentServer.asp? (accessed August 19, 2018).

[15] Ibid., 502.

[16] See "God Who Curses is Cursed: Recasting Imprecation in Africa," *Journal of Law, Religion and State* 6 (2018): 29-48.

helps us in our weakness; for we do not know how to pray as we ought, but that very Spirit intercedes with sighs too deep for words. And God, who searches the heart, knows what is the mind of the Spirit, because the Spirit intercedes for the saints according to the will of God."[17] According to Martin Luther, "God takes the initiative and puts into our mouths the very words and approach we are to use [in prayer]."[18] Prayer is a privilege as well as a responsibility, which God has given us as his priests by virtue of our baptism. Prayer accords us with the privilege to fulfill our priestly responsibility of approaching God by ourselves, with and for other Christians in faith. We pray not because we are worthy, but because we pray with confidence and faith in God. Unworthiness is a motivation rather than an obstacle to prayer! As Luther argues,

> We pray after all because we are unworthy to pray. The very fact that
> we are unworthy and that we dare to pray confidently, trusting only in the
> faithfulness of God, makes us worthy to pray and to have our prayer
> answered. . . . Your worthiness does not help you; and your unworthiness
> does not hinder you. Mistrust condemns you; but confidence makes you
> worthy and upholds you.[19]

For Luther, prayer is one of the marks of the true Church. Luther insists that the Church should never meet together, however briefly, without preaching of the word and prayer. "For indeed, the Christian church on earth has no greater power or work against everything that may oppose it than such common prayer."[20]

Nonetheless, prayer is the most distinguishing spiritual practice of every religion, it is not something peculiar to the Christian religion. The ritual of prayer is supposed to be a private encounter between an individual

---

[17] Romans 8:26-27, NRSV.

[18] Martin Luther, "The Large Catechism," in *The Book of Concord: The Confessions of the Evangelical Lutheran Church*, edited by Robert Kolb and Timothy Wengert (Minneapolis: Fortress Press, 2000), 443.

[19] Martin Luther, "On Rogationtide Prayer and Procession, 1519;" in *Luther's Works* 42, edited by Martin O. Dietrich and Helmut T. Lehmann (Philadelphia: Fortress Press, 1969), 89.

[20] Martin Luther, "A Treatise on Good Works, 1520," in *Luther's Works* 44, edited by James Atkinson and Helmut T. Lehmann (Philadelphia: Fortress Press, 1966), 66.

and God in virtue of the teaching of Jesus Christ. "Whenever you pray, do not be like the hypocrites; for they love to stand and pray in the synagogues and at the street corners, so that they may be seen by others. Truly I tell you, they have received their reward. But whenever you pray, go into your room and shut the door and pray to your Father who is in secret; and your Father who sees in secret will reward you."[21]

Yet, as a multi-religious society, prayer occupies a central place in both private and public life of Nigerians. Prayer has assumed a public dimension in Nigeria as Nigerians seek to live out their religious faith in public. They believe that religion is more than private affair. It impacts every department of their public life. Thus, prayer which is at the heart of religion has been accorded enormous significance beyond the confines of the church and mosque to embrace every aspect of our public life.

There is a place of worship in virtually every public and private institution where people of faith meet daily for prayer. Payer is also featured on the agenda of most public meetings and political rallies. Most formal public meetings in Nigeria begin and end with whether a Christian or Muslim prayer. The culture of praying in public places including at government functions is deeply entrenched in the psyche of Nigerian people. Any attempt at eliminating it is often met with severe resistance. Nigerians are "notorious" to borrow John Mbiti's word for praying in public, even though it is not always a reflection of a genuine piety. No doubt they are fond of blocking public roads during hours of such public prayer, which infringes on the rights of the public to freedom of movement.

At any rate, public prayer is a public practice of faith that fosters the relationship between the Church and the state. It legitimizes the state and publicizes the Church. As we shall see later, they both need prayer to approach each other and relate with God who establishes and sustains them in the world. God's sovereignty means that we are responsible to serve God, but the devil is still doing his work in high places - which can cause evil and oppression of innocent people. And prayer is an active process of

---

[21] Matthew 7:5-6.

asking God to intervene and to overcome the evil, even if it can win over us in our time on earth. As we shall see later, God is the source of political power, but has allowed some of that power to be exercised by forces of evil in the hand of human beings. And God has also commissioned us to stand for Him against that evil in public space.

THEOLOGICAL BASIS FOR POLITICAL PRAYER

Nigeria is a deeply religious society, even though its religiosity often has an inconsequential positive impact on its political public life. There is often a glaring disconnect between the religious faith that Nigerians profess and the life they live in public office.[22] Nonetheless, the existence of numerous places of worship in every part of Nigeria including public offices is an enough evidence to substantiate the inherent religiosity of the Nigerian people. The theological foundation of political prayer request in the Church is rooted in God as the ultimate source and dispenser of political leadership. God is the archetype and source of political power. All public political power has its ultimate origin in God.

Thus, politicians believe that political power must not only be derived, but also received from God for it to be legitimate and authoritative. The implication is that political leaders are stewards of public trust and power, which is delegated to them by God through the people. They are expected to use it for the common good of the public. Those who desire to acquire political power must first and foremost enlist the approval and endorsement of God through prayer, believing that God alone is who gives power to whoever God wills. God is believed to have a stake in anyone's electoral victory. God is who chooses political leaders in politics as a prominent politician and governor, Nasir El-Rufai claims. "In politics. . . .

---

[22] See "An 'Absence of God' from Public Life? The Disconnect between Faith and Life in the Church in Nigeria," *Word & World* 33, no. 3 (2013): 248-256.

Whoever you selected, is the choice of God."[23] God is thus the king maker of political leadership because God is he who ordains it from the foundation of the world.[24] Through attributing to God the power to ordain political leadership, St. Paul politicizes God's spiritual power in the world. Consequently, as we shall see later, he insists that it is right and acceptable to God for the Church to offer prayer for those in positions of leadership that they may work for peace and tranquility of the world.

Again, the adherent of every religion, including politicians running for public office, has a strong belief in the power of prayer to grant political power. Politicians who have such an unwavering belief in the power of God (whom the Church worships) to answer prayer would always delightfully run to the church for prayers in their struggle to seize political power. They believe that the Church is a spiritual gathering of righteous believers and that the "prayer of the righteous [people] is powerful and effective."[25] When the people of God offer prayer in unison and in faith for any noble cause they agree on, these politicians believe that God would answer the Church and grant the desired request. Of course, one of such noble causes that God is so pleased to respond to through prayer is the desire of politicians to capture public office! The politicians believe that through prayer God will cause the electorate to vote for them and grant them victory over their opponents.

There is no doubt a soft institutional separation between Church and politics in Nigeria. But prayer, which is the fundamental ritual of the Church, is the bridge between the two institutions. As the neutral platform, prayer is the medium through which God and humans, the sacred and the profane, politics and religion meet and mutually impacts each other. Prayer binds the Church and state together in unbounded relationships and in many ways shapes the functions of both. As the common means of approaching God through Jesus Christ, prayer has the power to draw politicians and clergy together to the common sacred space of the Church.

---

[23] Wale Odunsi, "APC: El-Rufai Vows to Remove Shehu Sani from Senate despite Meeting with Buhari," *Daily Post*, http://dailypost.ng/2018/08/26/apc-el-rufai-vows-remove-shehu-sani-senate-despite-meeting-buhari/ (accessed August 27, 2018).

[24] See Romans 13:1-7.

[25] James 5:16.

Thus, by asking the church leaders to pray for and with them for realizing their political dreams, politicians make their intentions to run for public office publicly known not only to the Church, but also to God. Politicians' claim to be religious as evidenced in their tactics of engaging in prayerful campaign in the sacred space of the Church is intended to accomplish such a publicity. This strategy is a powerful political tool that politicians utilize to gain the "favor" of the church and by extension, God.

But prayer in and of itself does not give any politicians control over state power and resources. God alone grants that. God reserves the prerogative to grant political leadership to anybody with or without our prayer. Though we can challenge such a divine prerogative in our prayer, we must recognize that God is not accountable to us for the way God exercises his sovereign power. God is always free to act as he wills without being answerable to us. Though God alone gives political power to whoever God's will with or without our prayer, God does not usually desire to do it apart from our prayer, the divine means by which God accomplishes his will for his believers in the world. God usually desires and enlists their prayers before meeting any of their human needs, including their needs to occupy political position.

PAULINE DIVINIZATION OF POLITICAL POWER AND POLITICIZATION OF PRAYER

Prayer was the central element of worship in the early Church. Prayer was largely a spiritual ritual performed essentially for enacting and re-enacting communion between God and his community of believers. It undergirded and permeated the entire spiritual life of the early Church. As a way of life, the apostles engaged in prayer unceasingly. John Abraham Godson writes, "The early Church had incessancy in their prayers. They prayed at all times, in every situation. Prayer was their lifeline, their source of strength."[26] The early Church was a praying community, they engaged fervently in praying for and with one another and above all to God through Jesus Christ. Apostle Luke reports that the early Church not only "continued with one accord in prayer,"[27] but also "continued steadfastly in the apostles' doctrine and fellowship, in the breaking of bread, and in prayers."[28] Even in the face of severe persecution that threatened the very foundation of the existence of the early Church, the believers never faltered in their prayer life. They insisted on boldly "praying and singing hymns to God."[29]

The motivation of prayer was largely spiritually rooted in the early Church devoid of any politics. The early believers engaged in prayer to accomplish spiritual goals. Through the power of prayer, they not only proclaimed the forgiveness of sin and imparted the Holy Spirit, but also ordained leaders and commissioned missionaries via laying on hands. Again, the early Church offered prayer for healing of the sick and for the deliverance of those who were held captive by demons and evil spirits. God was seen at work in their prayer, wreaking signs and wonders in Jesus name. Prayer was so profoundly significant in the spiritual life and faith of the early Church that the believers jealously protected it from any distractions such as serving the tables. The role that prayer played in the spiritual edification of the life of the believers necessitated the setting up of a committee of spirit-filled believers saddled with the ministry of serving the tables while the body of Christ invested its time and energy continually into prayer and the ministry of the word.[30]

But what we find in the later life of the early Church was the politicization of this solemn ritual of worship. In many ways, apostle Paul is guilty of this secularization of prayer. He takes this sacred ritual used primarily for spiritual ends and politicizes it when he divinizes the powers of civil government and calls on the Church to intercede for its leaders. He

[26] John Abraham Godson, "Prayer in the Early Church," *Lausanne World Purse Archives*, http://www.lausanneworldpulse.com/themedarticles-php/1480/12-2011 (accessed July 22, 2018).
[27] Acts 1:14, NKJV.
[28] Acts 2:42.
[29] Acts 16:25.
[30] Acts 6:4.

enjoins the Church to pray to God for not only spiritual, but also political ends. Paul's travails in the hands of political leaders of his day might have been responsible for this paradigm shift.

In particular, Paul assigns divine power to political leaders, characterizing them as God's representatives, ministers who wield the sword to reward the good and punish the evil to maintain peace and security in the world. He warns the Church against resisting political leaders, for such rebellion constitutes a resistance to God's own ordination. Thus, Paul implores the Church to submit to political powers which exist in the world in virtue of divine institution.[31] In other words, he believes that the obedience of the Church to human government is an obedience to God! For this cause, he contends that Christians must pay taxes and tributes to the government, but also pray for its leaders. As he writes, "First of all, then, I urge that supplications, prayers, intercessions, and thanksgivings be made for everyone, for kings and all who are in high positions, so that we may lead a quiet and peaceable life in all godliness and dignity. This is right and is acceptable in the sight of God our Savior."[32] The early Church carried out Paul's instruction with every diligence and faithfulness that they insisted or persisted in praying for civil authorities even under severe persecution.[33]

Paul believes that God is the foundation of state peace and security, which political leadership is divinely established in the world to provide and maintain for people to enjoy God's provision of comprehensive daily bread in peace.[34] The people cannot dutifully worship God, propagate the gospel, and engage in the lawful business of creating jobs, and of producing goods and services without peace and security. But unless God provides for such public peace and security political leaders will labor in vain to protect life and property. Therefore, political leaders must rely on God, the ultimate "chief security" of the world, in the discharge of their primary responsibility for maintaining peace and security. Without God the

---

[31] Romans 13:1-7.

[32] See 1 Timothy 2: 1-3, even though Pauline authorship of this epistle is contentious.

[33] See Tertullian, *Apology*, 30.

[34] See Ibrahim S. Bitrus, "Give Us Today Our Daily Bread: Martin Luther's Theology of Prosperity," in *Journal of Theology for Southern Africa* 160 (2018): 21-39.

author of just peace and security they are nothing and can't accomplish anything. They would rather be Satan's ministers of injustice and oppression than God's instruments of justice without which there would never be sustainable just peace. "When the righteous are in authority, the people rejoice; but when the wicked rule, the people groan."[35] In some sense, when the people of God do God's will, God can reward the people by giving them good leader, or good kings, but when the people disobey, then God gives them horrible leaders or kings.... and things fall apart. I am also tempted to think, there are other times when even good people are given horrible kings against whom they cannot resist. Paul is not unaware of this danger. He would not ignore the threat without jeopardizing the gospel of peace that he wanted to propagate. In Paul's estimation, political leaders cannot effectively restrain the forces of evil that obstruct peace and security which causes war and conflict in the world unless they themselves experience God's own protection from these evil forces through our fervent prayer. They need God to grant them inner peace and strength before they can provide just peace to the people!

Furthermore, the politicians who govern are God's servants called to serve public good which God has entrusted to them rather than themselves. They need wisdom, counsel, and a discerning heart to do their job of making and enforcing just laws and policies that improve the life of the people effectively, faithfully, and diligently. The job is a Herculean one that must not be taken for granted. The need for God to bestow political leaders with the Solomonic wisdom to lead the people with justice and mercy cannot be overstressed. Unless secular leaders exercise the fear of God which is the foundation of wisdom and wise government, they cannot deliver just and merciful public service. There is absolutely nothing wrong with Paul asking Church to pray for civil leaders especially those who lack wisdom to govern so that God may grant them the wisdom they so desired to rule with justice and righteousness. Politicians also need maintain high moral standards and integrity of character, which is a key factor in earning

---

[35] Proverbs 29:2. NRSV.

and maintaining public trust and delivering of quality political services to the public. All of these needs may not be met devoid of grace from above.

Those in power will run the risk of serving their own interests or that of sponsors rather than the common good without divine empowerment through prayer. The temptation to abuse power for personal gain by those who occupy public office is pretty strong and difficult to resist. They direly need prayer to overcome this temptation so as to remain true and faithful to their oath of office. Paul knows these felt needs of political leaders full well. He believes that God has the power to meet these much-desired needs of political leaders through prayer of faith. In the words Luther, "To pray... is to call upon God in every need."[36]

Above all, the Political leaders whether they are Christians or not for whom Paul encourages us to prayer are under God's sovereign power. Paul believes that as servants of God, there is no way they can escape from the sovereign control and judgement of God. His appeal to the Church to pray for those in corridors of power is grounded in God's absolute sovereignty over their lives. Paul Borthwick submits, "Prayer for political leaders flows from a perspective built on the foundation of the sovereignty of God. We pray believing that the whole earth is under his sovereign control. He is the Lord of history – past, present, and future. The people in positions of leadership are incorporated into his sovereign plan."[37] As sovereign Lord of nations and kingdoms of this world, God is he who holds and shapes the destiny of their political leaders. God has power to enthrone and overthrow them as he wills, albeit through human agency. As such any faithful prayer which invokes God to exercise such a sovereign power over political leaders will not be futile. In answer to the prayer of his people, God can change the worldly leaders even despotic ones to execute justice, but also restrain them from perpetrating injustice. Therefore, Paul's appeals to the Church to pray for political leaders is quite legitimate and appropriate. One

---

[36] Martin Luther, "The Small Catechism," in *The Book of Concord: The Confessions of the Evangelical Lutheran Church*, edited by Robert Kolb and Timothy Wengert (Minneapolis: Fortress Press, 2000), 443.

[37] Paul Borthwick, *"Praying for Political Leaders,"* https://daintl.org.uk/wp-content/uploads/2015/05/Praying-for-Political-Leaders-Paul-Borthwick-v2.pdf (accessed July 22, 2018).

must totally understand and sympathize with Paul's earnest call on us to intercede for those who govern us.

But through linking prayer with political power and divinizing the latter, Paul bridges the gap between politics and religion, formally collapsing the wall separating the two institutions.[38] He spiritualizes political power, while politicizing prayer. In virtue of this, the Church enters the political realm of the state and vice versa, the state enters the spiritual realm of the Church. I would argue that it was not Emperor Constantine who first Christianized state power and politicized the Church in the history of Christianity. Paul was the first Christian scholar and theologian who accomplished it at least in theory. Constantine simply perfected, applied, and institutionalized the religio-political ground-plan of Paul.

THE CHURCH AS A NEUTRAL PUBLIC SPACE FOR POLITICAL PRAYER

The power of political prayer must not be underestimated. Political prayer often wields double-edged power. It has the power not only to enthrone political leaders, but also the power to dethrone them. The Church is arguably the most neutral sacred public space where this power of political prayer is exercised even though the Church is supposed to be an apolitical institution, which does not belong to any political party nor does its clergy publicly endorse any candidate for political position. To begin with, the Church by virtue of its spiritual constitution is a house of prayer. Jesus wouldn't have minced words with claiming the Church as his Father's house of prayer, where the saints gather together to listen to preaching and offer sacrifice of praise and worship to God. Just as Jewish religious leaders tuned the synagogue, a house of prayer, into the den of robbers, politicians in Nigeria have turned the church into a political

---

[38] Indeed, in Christ, nothing is not spiritual or secular. All secular things are also spiritual from God's point of view. God is not a dualist. We can be so.

campaign trail. But the political neutrality of the Church as an institution is what makes the Church a fertile public space conducive for such a "religio-political" activity. This is not to say that every church member and leader is politically neutral in public matters of political importance. But as a nonpartisan institution, the Church often brings card-carrying members of different political parties together to worship with one another regardless of their political affiliations. The divergent political ideologies and loyalties which often divide people into antagonistic political factions in the society barely find expression in the Church.

Second, the Church is also arguably the most neutral public space in Nigeria where the Spirit gathers up people of diverse ethnic nationalities together to worship God in truth and in spirit. Though these people may have different ethnic loyalties, in Christ they stand in love and unity with one another in the Church of God. Though the Church as a multi-ethnic ethnic community more often than experiences ethnic tensions and animosity, this ethnic strife does not de-neutralize it as a sacred public space. It still stands out clearly as a nonpartisan fertile ground for politicians of diverse religious faiths and backgrounds to express their political imaginations. This execution expresses itself in the politicians' declaration of their intentions to run for public office under pretext of seeking prayer from the church.

Moreover, the church commands one of the largest followings in Nigeria. Though accurate data on the membership of the two dominant religious groups—Christianity and Islam—are not easy to come by, one can pontificate without exaggeration that the church constitutes more than 50 percent of the Nigerian's total population. The crowds which the Spirit gathers up on every Sunday to pray, to listen to sermon, and celebrate the sacraments in churches across Nigeria arguably outnumber the crowds often gathered at any political campaign rallies. Political aspirants who hunt for large crowds to sale their manifesto cannot ignore the Church without putting their electoral success at risk. As a result, they would often avail themselves of every available human and moral avenues within their reach to woo the support of the church. This often requires politicians giving monetary donations to the church, but most importantly beseeching the church to pray for the attainment of their political ambition.

The most compelling reason is that the church leaders often wield enormous political influence in virtue of their authority and positions in the church and society, even though they are called primarily to be ministers of the word and sacraments. Their commission to faithfully preach the word of God invests in them the prophetic authority to speak truth to power. As prophet Jeremiah, God has appointed them "over nations and over kingdoms, to pluck up and to pull down, to destroy and to overthrow, to build and to plant."[39] Many of them have exercised their prophetic power to influence directly or indirectly government policy and decisions, but also to impact the political behavior and choice of their members. As powerful prophetic public opinion leaders, Church leaders have played a powerful role in articulating publicly constructive criticism of government in power. As a matter of fact, they have even called for the immediate resignation of the government in power due to its apparent failure in safeguarding life and property its citizens. A quick analysis of the current situation in the country is sufficient to substantiate my claim.

The Nigerian economy has been in shambles since the current administration took power. The national currency, the naira has experienced the most dismal depreciation in the history of the country. Life has become unbearable for the average Nigerian. The problem of insecurity has worsened and even aggravated with the senseless destruction of life and property of innocent Nigerians by the terror groups such as the Boko Haram and the Fulani herdsmen. The Christian Church and communities in the Middle Belt region are most impacted by this organized violence and terrorism perpetrated with the connivance of those in government. According to the former minister of defense, Gen T. Y. Danjuma (retired), the Nigerian armed forces are aiding and abetting the attacks on the minority ethnic nationalities and Christian communities by the armed terror groups in Nigeria. "The armed forces are not neutral. They collude with the armed bandits that kill people, kill Nigerians. They

---

[39] Jeremiah 1:10. NRSV.

facilitate their movement. They cover them." Danjuma warns "If you are depending on the armed forces to stop the killings, you will die one by one."[40]

The impact of this persistent violence on the church in northern Nigeria is enormous. According to the Open Doors International, between 2006 and 2014 an estimated "12,500 Christians have been killed, over 550,000 Christians are displaced, and 13,000 churches are destroyed or abandoned."[41] As the fourth most dangerous terror group in the world, the Fulani herdsmen have killed more than three thousand Christians, including two catholic priests since 2015 to this day. The massive failure of state actors to fully guarantee the security of life and property in the country has led many church leaders and Christian associations to raise their public prophetic voices more than ever before not only against the government, but also in defense of their members.

Outraged by the barbaric killing of two catholic priests and their fifteen parishioners while celebrating mass in the church by Fulani herdsmen, Catholic Bishops Conference of Nigeria issued a prophetic public statement passing vote of no confidence on the security agencies of the government. The catholic bishops indicted not only the heads of the security agencies of complicity in the killing, but also the president of refusing to hold them accountable. For failing to protect the life and property of his citizens from the bloodshed that threatens the foundation of the collective existence and unity of Nigeria, the catholic hierarchies bluntly told the president, "it is time for him to choose the part of honour and consider stepping aside to save the nation from total collapse."[42]

---

[40] Magaji Isa Hunkuyi, "Military colluding with Armed bandits – TY Danjuma," *Daily Trust,* https://www.dailytrust.com.ng/military-colluding-with-armed-bandits-ty-danjuma.html (accessed August 4, 2018).

[41] Christian Association of Nigeria, "Crushed but not Defeated, The Impact of Persistent Violence on the Church in Northern Nigeria," *Open Doors International,* https://www.opendoors.pl/sites/default/files/Open_Doors_Nigeria_Kampagne_Report.pdf (accessed August 19, 2018).

[42] Catholic Bishops Conference of Nigeria, "When Will this Barbarism End?" A Statement Issued by the Catholic Bishops' Conference in the Wake of the Murder of Two Priests and their Parishioners during the Celebration of the Holy Mass, in Mbalom, Benue State, April 25, 2018.

Bishop Samuel Ezeofor also criticizes the ruling party, the APC for disappointing Nigerians by falling deliver its campaign promises. He enjoins to Nigerians to abandon the ruling party before the forthcoming national elections and join to any party that would promote and advance the progress and development of Nigeria. According to Ezeofor,

> "APC has moved us backward and if we must progress, we must do the needful by leaving the APC which could not lead Nigeria to the promised land and queue behind a party that can guarantee our progress because we must progress as a nation since Nigeria is bigger than a single individual or APC as a political party."[43]

The prophetic criticism of any government of the day, in which church leaders point to its weaknesses to problematize its existence, but also suggest a credible alternative government, has capacity to influence political behavior and decision of their followers. Such a critical prophetic criticism can inspire the people to rise against any government in power. This may inspire the people to engage in a public protest against the government or vote an opposition political party into power or do both to express their popular disenchantment with the government. Recently for example, the Christians in Nigeria in compliance with the prophetic call of the Christian Association of Nigerian (CAN), embarked on a nationwide prophetic protest march against the rampant bloodletting perpetrated by Fulani militia groups and armed herdsmen across the country. During the prophetic protest, the CAN audaciously called on the president to end the violence or forget his re-election bid.

> "We have lost faith in the security agencies and they must sack all the security chiefs and replace them with new ones. No more bloodshed; if the bloodshed continues, this administration should forget about 2019. We cannot continue like this. Enough is enough."[44]

---

[43] Nwabueze Okonkwo, "2019: Forget about APC, Anglican Bishop Tells Nigerians," *Vanguard*, https://www.vanguardngr.com/2018/08/2019-forget-about-apc-anglican-bishop-tells-nigerians/ (accessed August 3, 2018).

[44] Oluseye Ojo et al, CAN Tells Buhari to Forget 2019, *The Sun*, http://sunnewsonline.com/can-tells-buhari-to-forget-2019/ (accessed August 9, 2018).

As I write this chapter, Adamawa state Christians in response to the prophetic directive of their state CAN have just staged a peaceful prophetic procession to the government house of the state to protest against the recurring attacks by the Fulani herdsmen on predominantly Christian communities in the state. Thousands of people participated in the public prophetic procession. The CAN demanded the government in its letter to the president (delivered to the deputy governor at the end of the procession) to put an immediate end to the attacks, bring the perpetrators to justice and restore total peace in the affected communities.[45]

But the church leaders can equally sing praises for the government in power, publicizing its achievements to legitimize its existence, and insisting on its continuity in power. For example, a group of Northern Pastors under the umbrella of Arewa Pastors Peace Initiative, Nigeria, APPIN contends that the people who criticize president Buhari for executing the agenda of Islamizing Nigeria are disgruntled elements of the opposition bent on discrediting his government. The pastors promise to deal squarely with their colleagues who are used by the opposition to cause mayhem in the country through promoting hate speech from the altar of the Church. The group also commends the president for providing excellent leadership in revamping the economy, tackling insecurity and transforming the agricultural sector.[46]

Similarly, the President, Christ Apostolic Church (CAC) Worldwide, Pastor Abraham Akinosun, who urges Christians to stop criticizing president Buhari, says they should rather pray for him. "Leaders fail when people fail to pray. Stop abusing and cursing our leaders because as you curse them the consequences will be borne by all citizens. If we pray for our leaders, God will inspire them [,] and everything will be all right."[47] Implied by these comments is that the prophetic power of church leaders to approve of any government in power, and even to oppose forces that may

---

[45] CAN, "Adamawa State Christians Demand an End to Mindless Massacre of Innocent Citizens," Letter to the President, August 1, 2018.

[46] See "Photos: Buhari and Northern Pastor's Forum Meeting," *Vanguard*, https://www. vanguardngr.com/2018/04/969428/ (accessed August 10, 2018).

[47] "Stop Complaining, Pray for Buhari, CAC President Tells Christians," *Vanguard*, https:// www.vanguardngr.com/2018/04/stop-complaining-pray-buhari-cac-president-tells-christian s/ (accessed August 10, 2018).

bring about change of power. The commendation may encourage their members to follow suit by supporting the government in power and exercising their franchise in the next election in favor of the government. Therefore, no political aspirants would dare undermine the prophetic power and authority of the clergy to influence the political behavior of their members and the public in their quest for seizing state power and get away with it. Politicians would dearly pay for it should they do that. Thus, they just need the spiritual and moral support of the clergy through prayer not only to capture political power, but also to succeed in leading the people in peace.

The last but not the least in weight point is that as an inherently religious society, Nigerians generally desire to be led by politicians who are godly or those who claim to be religious or identify themselves with a particular religion. It would be impossible for politicians who openly identify themselves as atheists or the "nones" to run and win public office in Nigeria. To circumvent this stumbling block to acquisition of state power, the politicians have no option but to demonstrate publicly their religiosity. As Matthew Kukah argues, "no one can aspire to, or hold political office in Nigeria without pretending to be religious."[48] Participating in the ritual of the church such as worship and prayer, but also in contributing whether in cash or kind to the growth and development of the church is a tangible proof of the politicians' religiosity.

But the politicians' participation in the affairs of the church knows no denominational boundaries or even religious affiliations when it comes to these politicians campaigning for political office. They often are willing to go to any length, including crossing all denominational lines and religious boundaries in their religious participation to demonstrate to the public their religious inclusiveness. This quality of inclusion is a critical factor for determining the competency and suitability of political aspirants in a multi-religious society like Nigeria. In fact, an exemplified quality religious inclusivity (even if in theory) is an essential sine qua non for politicians to garner popular political support. For example, to convince Christians that

---

[48] Matthew Hassan Kukah, *Religion, Politics and Power in Northern Nigeria* (Ibadan: Spectrum Books, 1993), 228.

he is a religious inclusivist rather than an Islamic bigot and fanatic, Buhari, a Muslim who was the 2015 APC presidential aspirant did not only to pick a pastor his running mate, he also attended a Christian thanksgiving worship service at RCCG.[49] This underscores the desire that Nigerians want to have as political leaders who are not religious bigots or at least those who do not appear to be religious extremists. They yearn for political leaders who live above religious bigotry and epitomize a significant political sensitive to the feelings and aspirations of all religions.

In many ways, the church in Nigeria operates an open-door policy that welcomes all politicians who come to their sacred spaces and to submit their prayer request to vie for public office without of discrimination. The commitment of the church to providing neutral platform to all political aspirants irrespective of their political parties and religious beliefs to enlist its spiritual support is profound and unwavering. This unshakable commitment largely constrains the church from turning down prayer requests from any politician. It also compels the church to do an incredible job of giving fair and equal attention, treatment and opportunity to all political aspirants.

CONCLUSION

I have established that there is a significant relationship between prayer and the pursuit of state power and resources in the church. The one penetrates and is penetrated by the other in the sacred public space of the Church. They mutually interact and impact the public functions of each other in the process of capturing and maintaining control over state power and sharing of public resources. Politicians use prayer as a powerful spiritual resource for campaigning for the support of the church and by extension, endorsement of God. The Christian Church particularly its leaders deploy prayer to exercise their prophetic authority and influence

---

[49] "Buhari Attend Annual Lagos Thanksgiving Service," *Daily Post*, http://dailypost.ng/2015/01/04/buhari-attends-annual-lagos-thanksgiving-service-photos/ (accessed August 18, 2018.).

over politicians in their quest for public office and running the affairs of
the government. The church leaders also deploy political prayer for
personal enrichment, but also for the promotion of the common good of the
church and society as a whole. As power brokers, they have come to play a
strategic role in the Nigerian politics wielding enormous influence in the
church and society.

REFERENCES

Albert, Isaac Olawale. 2007. "A Review of the Campaign Strategies."
    Journal of African Elections 6: 55-78.

Bible, NRSV.

Bible, NKJV.

Bitrus, Ibrahim S. 2013. "An 'Absence of God' from Public Life? The
    Disconnect between Faith and Life in the Church in Nigeria." *Word &
    World* 33: 248-256.

———— 2018. "God Who Curses is Cursed: Recasting Imprecation in
    Africa." *Journal of Law, Religion and State* 6: 29-48.

Borthwick, Paul. *Praying for Political Leaders*. Accessed July 22, 2018.
    https://daintl.org.uk/wp-content/uploads/2015/05/Praying-for-Political-
    Leaders-Paul-Borthwick-v2.pdf.

Bratton, Micheal. 2008. "Voting Buying and Violence in Nigerian Election
    Campaigns." *Afrobarometer*: 1-21. Accessed August 19, 2018.
    https://www.files.ethz.ch/isn/91313/AfropaperNo99.pdf.

"Buhari Attend Annual Lagos Thanksgiving Service." *Daily Post*.
    Accessed August 18, 2018. http://dailypost.ng/2015/01/04/buhari-
    attends-annual-lagos-thanksgiving-service-photos/.

CAN, *Adamawa State Christians Demand an End to Mindless Massacre of
    Innocent Citizens*, Letter to the President, August 1, 2018.

Catholic Bishops Conference of Nigeria, *When Will this Barbarism End?*
    A Statement Issued by the Catholic Bishops' Conference in the Wake
    of the Murder of Two Priests and their Parishioners during the

Celebration of the Holy Mass, in Mbalom, Benue State, April 25, 2018.

Christian Association of Nigeria, "Crushed but not Defeated, The Impact of Persistent Violence on the Church in Northern Nigeria." *Open Doors International*. Accessed August 19, 2018. https://www.opendoo rs.pl/sites/default/files/Open_Doors_Nigeria_Kampagne_Report.pdf.

Odunsi, Wale. "APC: El-Rufai Vows to Remove Shehu Sani from Senate Despite Meeting with Buhari." *Daily Post*. Accessed August 27, 2018. http://dailypost.ng/2018/08/26/apc-el-rufai-vows-remove-shehu-sani-senate-despite-meeting-buhari/.

Ekhareafo, Daniel Ofomegbe, and Akoseogasimhe, Isaac Michael. 2017 "A Textual Analysis of 2015 Presidential Election Advertisements in Selected Nigerian Newspapers." *MCC* 1:149-177.

"Election: Pastor Bakare Challenges Christian Church Over Political Support, Alleges Some Pastors Sold Their Conscience In 2011." *Sahara Reporters*. Accessed August 15, 2015. http://saharareporters. com/ 2015/ 01/ 06/ election-pastor-bakare-challenges-christian-church-over-political-support-alleges-some.

Godson, John Abraham. "Prayer in the Early Church." *Lausanne World Purse Archives*, Accessed July 22, 2018. http://www.lausanneworld pulse.com/themedarticles-php/1480/12-2011.

Hunkuyi, Magaji Isa. "Military colluding with Armed bandits – TY Danjuma." *Daily Trust*. Accessed August 4, 2018. https://www.daily trust.com.ng/military-colluding-with-armed-bandits-ty-danjuma.html.

Interview with Rev Benedict Barde Cham. August 19, 2018.

Kukah, Matthew Hassan.1993. *Religion, Politics and Power in Northern Nigeria*. Ibadan: Spectrum Books.

Luther, Martin. 2000. "The Small Catechism." In *The Book of Concord: The Confessions of the Evangelical Lutheran Church*, edited by Robert Kolb and Timothy Wengert. Minneapolis: Fortress Press.

_____ 2000. "The Large Catechism." In *The Book of Concord: The Confessions of the Evangelical Lutheran Church*, edited by Robert Kolb and Timothy Wengert. Minneapolis: Fortress Press.

_____ 1969. "On Rogationtide Prayer and Procession, 1519." In *Luther's Works* 42, edited by Martin O. Dietrich and Helmut T. Lehman. Philadelphia: Fortress Press.

_____ "A Treatise on Good Works, 1520." In *Luther's Works* 44, edited by James Atkinson and Helmut T. Lehman. Philadelphia: Fortress Press.

Ojekwe. Grace Izeghe. *Political Advert Campaigns and Voting Behaviour: A Study of Akinwunmi Ambode's Election Ad Campaigns in Lagos State.* Accessed August 3, 2018. http://www.inecnigeria.org/wp-content/uploads/2015/07/Conference-Paper-by-Grace-Ojekwe.pdf.

Ojo, Oluseye, etal. "CAN Tells Buhari to Forget 2019." *The Sun.* Accessed August 9, 2018. http://sunnewsonline.com/can-tells-buhari-to-forget-2019/.

Okekere, Samuel. *Why Nigerian Pastors Should Stop Allowing Politicians to Campaign Inside Churches.* Accessed August 14, 2018. Naija Gists.com, https://naijagists.com/why-nigerian-pastors-should-stop-allowing-politicians-to-campaign-inside-churches/.

Okonkwo, Nwabueze. "2019: Forget about APC, Anglican Bishop Tells Nigerians." *Vanguard.* Accessed August 3, 2018. https://www. vanguardngr.com/ 2018/ 08/ 2019-forget-about-apc-anglican-bishop-tells-nigerians/.

Okonkwo, Oge. "Members of Popular Church 'Divided' over Jonathan's Visit." *Purse.* Accessed August 15, 2018. https://www.pulse.ng/ communities/ religion/ winners-chapel-members-of-popular-church-divided-over-jonathans-visit-id3438602.html.

"Photos: Buhari and Northern Pastor's Forum Meeting." *Vanguard.* Accessed August 10, 2018. https://www.vanguardngr.com/2018/04/969428/.

Rippentrop, Jan Schnell. 2017. "Marks Passion Narrative as Political Theology." *Currents in Theology and Mission* 44:11-19. Accessed August 19, 2018. https://content.ebscohost.com/ContentServer.asp?.

Shearer, Tobin Miller. 2015. "Invoking Crisis: Performative Christian Prayer and the Civil Rights Movement." *Journal of the American Academy of Religion* 83: 490-512.

"Stop Complaining, Pray for Buhari, CAC President Tells Christians." *Vanguard*. Accessed August 10, 2018. https://www.vanguardngr.com/2018/04/stop-complaining-pray-buhari-cac-president-tells-christians/.

Tertullian. *Apology*.

Wilmot, Patrick F. 1985. *Sociology: A New Introduction*. London: Collins International Textbooks.

"What Buhari Promised Nigerians." *Vanguard*. May 28, 2015. Accessed July 25, 2018. https://www.vanguardngr.com/2015/05/what-buhari-promised-nigerians/.

INDEX

The Political Economy of National and Energy Security

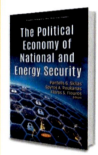

EDITOR: Pantelis Sklias, Spyros Roukanas, and Floros Flouros, MBA, MA, MSc, PhD candidate

SERIES: Energy Policies, Politics and Prices

BOOK DESCRIPTION: The aim of this collective volume is to study the crucial aspects related to the interconnection between the political economy of energy security and national security, which is of great importance globally, due to great volatility and complexity.

HARDCOVER ISBN: 978-1-53614-745-2
RETAIL PRICE: $230

Essays in Political Anthropology: Reviewing the Essence of Capitalism

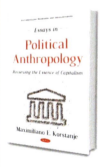

EDITOR: Maximiliano E. Korstanje

SERIES: Anthropology Research and Developments

BOOK DESCRIPTION: This book captivates the needs of discussing capitalism from a new angle, introducing new theories, insights and debates revolving around political anthropology.

SOFTCOVER ISBN: 978-1-53614-291-4
RETAIL PRICE: $82